Ontological and Imputed
Righteousness in Luther
and the Lutheran Confessions

Ontological and Imputed Righteousness in Luther and the Lutheran Confessions

Development of the Reformational Doctrine of Justification

HAROLD HOFSTAD

WIPF & STOCK · Eugene, Oregon

ONTOLOGICAL AND IMPUTED RIGHTEOUSNESS IN LUTHER
AND THE LUTHERAN CONFESSIONS
Development of the Reformational Doctrine of Justification

Copyright © 2025 Harold Hofstad. All rights reserved. Except for brief quotations in critical publications or reviews, no part of this book may be reproduced in any manner without prior written permission from the publisher. Write: Permissions, Wipf and Stock Publishers, 199 W. 8th Ave., Suite 3, Eugene, OR 97401.

Wipf & Stock
An Imprint of Wipf and Stock Publishers
199 W. 8th Ave., Suite 3
Eugene, OR 97401

www.wipfandstock.com

PAPERBACK ISBN: 979-8-3852-5436-1
HARDCOVER ISBN: 979-8-3852-5437-8
EBOOK ISBN: 979-8-3852-5438-5

12/09/25

Contents

Preface | vii

Abbreviations | ix

1. Introduction | 1
2. Background and Context for the Emergence of Luther's Theology | 11
   Luther's Own Account: The "Tower Experience" | 13
   Luther's Own Account: Law and Gospel | 15
   The Promise Communicated from God as the Gospel | 16
   Promise and Faith | 17
   Anfechtung and the Introspective Conscience | 19
   The Medieval Penitential System | 22
3. Components in Luther's Theology of Justification | 26
   Authoritative Basis | 28
   Direct Access and Reception | 29
   Forgiveness of Sin and Eternal Life | 30
   Unconditional Grace and Salvation | 32
   Independent of Renewal (the Order of Salvation) | 32
   Personal Certainty | 33
   Good Works as Fruits | 33
   Traditional Attempts to Actively Reach Salvation are Obsolete | 35
   Repentance as Sign of Free (Gifted) Salvation | 37

Contents

4 Influences, Interlocuters, and Developments | 38
  Peter Lombard, Gabriel Biel, and Anselm | 40
  Erasmus of Rotterdam | 43
  Augustine of Hippo | 47

5 Melanchthon and Luther | 52
  Early Work and Doctrine | 55
  The *Loci Communes* | 57

6 The Lutheran Confessions | 61
  Catechisms | 61
  The *Augsburg Confession* | 62
  The *Confutation of the Augsburg Confession* | 64
  The *Apology of the Augsburg Confession* | 64
  Between the Apology and the Formula | 66
  Andreas Osiander the Elder: A Different View of Justification | 67
  The *Formula of Concord* | 69

7 Ecumenical Considerations and Conclusions | 72
  The New Finnish Luther Scholarship and Interpretation | 72
  The *Joint Declaration on the Doctrine of Justification* | 78
  Conclusions | 82

Bibliography | 89

Preface

THIS BOOK TRACES THE development of Luther's thinking on justification, righteousness, and the role of faith, with special emphasis on pinpointing a definitive turning point on the way to arriving at a full reformational articulation. It shows how he evolved on this issue through his formative influences, collaborations, and controversies. Solidification of his interpretation by the Lutheran Confessional documents is illustrated. The book ends with conclusions about Lutheran theology with respect to justification, and potential progress on understanding made recently.

Abbreviations

AC	Augsburg Confession
ALC	American Lutheran Church
BC	*The Book of Concord: The Confessions of the Evangelical Lutheran Church.* Edited by Robert Kolb and Timothy J. Wengert. Translated by Charles Arand et al. Minneapolis: Fortress, 2000.
CR	Corpus Reformatorum
ELCA	Evangelical Lutheran Church in America
FC	Formula of Concord
JDDJ	*Joint Declaration on the Doctrine of Justification, 20th Anniversary Edition,* by the Lutheran World Federation and the Roman Catholic Church, (including statements from the World Methodist Council, the Anglican Consultative Council, and the World Communion of Reformed Churches). Geneva: The Lutheran World Federation, 2019.
LTSG	Lutheran Theological Seminary at Gettysburg
LW	Luther's Works, American Edition. Pelikan, Jaroslav, and Helmut Lehmann, eds. *Luther's Works, American Edition,* Vols. 1–55. St. Louis: Concordia and Minneapolis: Fortress, 1955–1986.
LWF	Lutheran World Federation

Abbreviations

ULS   United Lutheran Seminary

WA   Luther's Works, Weimar Edition. *D. Martin Luthers Werke*, Weimarer Ausgrebe, 65 vols. Weimar Bohlau, 1883–1993.

1

Introduction

MARTIN LUTHER IS NOT considered a systematic theologian, though he often thought systematically while conducting his work. Rather, he was a Bible teacher by profession—specifically, a professor of Old Testament at Wittenberg University. He approached theology somewhat in the way the Apostle Paul did in his occasional New Testament letters to fledgling Christian churches. In similar fashion, Luther responded to whatever issues came his way that he believed merited attention, as he addressed the ecclesiastical situation in sixteenth century Europe. He wrote, lectured, and preached profusely about many and varied things, as demonstrated by his voluminous corpus of works.

The one issue that dominated his thinking over all others was the doctrine of justification, which he considered "the article by which the Church stands or falls." For Luther, every other doctrine was ultimately related to that one. It seems that this doctrine either can't be captured and defined completely and comprehensively with finality by a systematic theology, or that theologians don't agree on its definition. My basic working definition of justification is: how a person can be put into a right relationship or have a right and acceptable standing with God. In the details of how this works, it continues to be a source of controversy and debate.

ONTOLOGICAL AND IMPUTED RIGHTEOUSNESS

Churches and theologians with a more confessional orientation are likely to feel that the controversies were already settled with the *Formula of Concord* (FC), which united feuding Lutheran theologians and factions near the end of the sixteenth century (1577). The publication of the *Book of Concord* (BC) (1580), which contained the FC, along with the other earlier documents widely in use and by then considered normative for Lutheran churches, was a milestone that solidified the teaching of those churches in Germany going forward. In the twentieth century, following the Luther renaissance in historical theological studies, and driven by an impetus from the ecumenical movement, controversy again emerged, specifically regarding the doctrine of justification, long considered to be at the very heart of Lutheran theology.

One of the most important modern challenges to traditional Lutheran theology is from the so-called new perspective on Paul, initiated by Ernst Käsemann and developed by Krister Stendahl, with subsequent contributions from others. Similarly to Dutch philosopher and theologian Desiderius Erasmus in the sixteenth century, they had come to view the historical context for the Apostle Paul's discussion of justification primarily as addressing the issue of Jewish-Gentile fellowship in the first century church, rather than as a solution for the existential psychological experience of guilt and the quest for certainty of salvation (as with Luther). While not negating Luther's interpretation of Paul (Paul assumed knowledge of justification on the part of his hearers and readers), these studies paved the way for some to view justification as historically conditioned by the experience of Luther and other reformers in the late medieval period, and as one doctrine among many, rather than the central teaching of the Church.

The other main challenge to the traditional confessional view of justification comes from the Finnish school of Luther studies spearheaded by Tuomo Mannermaa and his colleagues. In a way it isn't so surprising that this perspective came from Finland. Apart from the Church of Sweden, the Scandinavian Lutheran churches never subscribed to all documents in the BC. They generally accepted only the Augsburg Confession (AC), along with

Introduction

Luther's Small Catechism and Large Catechism. Later, Sweden adopted the BC officially, but the Finish church never did, not having experienced the intra-Lutheran conflicts of the Germans. Their modern context for interpreting Luther anew emerged from the Orthodox-Lutheran theological dialogs that took place in the twentieth century.

Robert Kolb observed that there are two main streams of thought in contemporary Lutheran theology concerning justification. One is driven primarily by an ecumenical agenda to find unity and agreement across denominations, while the other is driven by a confessional and historical approach to find contemporary application of Luther's insights.[1] I refer here to motivations rather than methods. Both perspectives may be grounded in historical and contextual approaches. I endeavor to take a historical approach in this thesis while being mindful of ecumenical developments and concerns as they bear upon the research undertaken herein. I investigate the implications of Finnish Luther studies, evaluating them against a backdrop of historical perspectives and contexts for the development of Lutheran theology, including the *Lutheran Confessions* as well as a selection of Luther's writing and lectures.

Considering the title of this thesis, *Ontological and Imputed Righteousness in Luther and the Lutheran Confessions*, some definitions are in order. "Imputed righteousness" or "forensic justification" refers to a forensic metaphor in which a sinner appearing before the Divine judge (God the Father), as if in a courtroom proceeding, is acquitted based on the innocence and divine obedience of another person, namely Jesus Christ. Christ's own righteousness (which is perfect and uniquely acceptable to God) is imputed or credited to the sinner, thereby erasing the guilt of sin. Faith, in this scenario, is conceived of as trust in this divine verdict and acquittal, making it effective. By way of contrast, "ontological righteousness" refers to inherent righteousness in the Christian believer as brought about by divine transformation. It is thought that faith and the action of the Holy Spirit bring about this transformation, and is at least part of what makes a sinner acceptable to God.

---

1. Kolb, *Contemporary Lutheran Understandings*, 154.

However, this leaves open the question of why the Incarnation of Christ was necessary and has implications for theories about the Atonement. It has been described by Catholic apologists as an inherent, real, and intrinsic righteousness rather than an extrinsic righteousness as characterized by the historic Protestant doctrine.[2] Forensic justification has been criticized as legal fiction, deficient, weak, and incomplete. Lutherans, for their part, have never denied an internal transformation resulting from justification, but have denied that this transformation is in any way the cause of justification or salvation. They have traditionally maintained that the order of salvation is justification first, then sanctification. In this view, sanctification will always be incomplete in earthly life and therefore cannot be the cause of justification. Some theologians have embraced an ontological perspective over (or in addition to) the traditional forensic model for justification and have discovered, during ecumenical dialog, an affinity with the Eastern Orthodox idea of theosis—as well as echoes in Lutheran theology. The idea of divinization is thought to be present in ancient creeds and in early theologians such as Irenaeus, Athanasius, and the Cappadocian Fathers, for example. Others have been suspicious that it represents a revival of "heretical" ideas about justification originating with Andreas Osiander in the sixteenth century—ideas that were firmly rejected and condemned by the FC. Factions that were otherwise contending with each other (Gnesio-Lutherans and Philipists) united against Osiander in the process of finalizing the FC. Still others have expressed the idea that the later theology of the *Lutheran Confessions* diverged from Luther, or that the older Luther diverged significantly from his own earlier Catholic, more Augustinian theology. Finally, attempts have been made to reconcile or synthesize the two viewpoints, for example, by joining the concepts of forensic justification with effective justification by citing Luther's statement that imputation perfects an incomplete or imperfect ontological righteousness,[3] or by asserting a future

2. Whalen, *Separated Brethren*, 20–21.
3. Gerrish, *Old Protestantism and the New*, 69–89.

Introduction

(eschatological or proleptic) ontological righteousness that is heralded by God's present forensic declaration of righteousness.[4]

Has there been a resurrection or at least a partial rehabilitation by the Finnish school of Osiander's theology, which featured ideas rejected by the FC? If so, what are the reasons? If not, why do their opponents think they have? I look at motivations for preferring one framework vs. another (ontological vs. forensic) and for preferring the perspective of either the younger or the older Luther's theology regarding justification, providing evidence from his writings that they differ. Support for the Finnish perspectives and opposition to them relate to ecumenical wishes, the threat to confessional identity, and potential compromises that either satisfy or do not satisfy those ecumenical wishes, along with desires to preserve the Lutheran theological tradition one way or another. The renewed interest in an ontological view (related to an indwelling Christ) may represent a softening of the historic confessional stance. Depending on the criteria, this may be considered good if it solves theological difficulties, enriches perspectives, or represents genuine progress in understanding, authenticity, and unity in the kerygmatic proclamation of the Church. Or it may be bad if it fosters forgetfulness and carelessness in doctrine, laxity in commitment, or loss of meaningful theological perspectives and helpful explanations that give the best and clearest comfort of the gospel. It may be that the Finnish theologians have simply provoked a more nuanced account and appreciation of Luther's theological development, and the development of Lutheran theology after Luther.

Articles have been published in theological journals and books either reacting in a negative, critical way to the Finnish school's theology in the context of a traditional confessional Lutheran stance, or in a positive way in appreciation of new insight into Luther's writings and for their potential as unifying perspectives in the project of enhancing ecumenical relations. A more detailed description is provided at the beginning of chapter 7. Others have argued forcefully in their publications and essays for a purely

---

4. Iwand, *Righteousness of Faith*, 76–80.

forensic model. A view has advanced in recent times that Luther's understanding of righteousness by faith is better characterized as a progressive series of insights developed in stages from his scriptural studies, culminating rather than beginning in a decisive breakthrough with the understanding of Rom 1:16–17 that Luther attributed to his "tower experience."[5]

My thesis is that Luther described justification both as forensic and as ontological, variously, depending upon the circumstance or theological issue at hand he was addressing, continuing in this fashion even after arriving at his reformational understanding. As time went on, however, he shifted to greater emphasis on imputation, as that approach provided greater clarity in his theological disputes. He was also influenced by Philip Melanchthon's thinking in this regard (see chapter 5). In either case, he maintained that the righteousness of God imparted to a person was alien and passive in character, coming from outside and appropriated solely through the instrumentality of faith. The confessional documents in the main reflect Luther's mature theology, though those involved in writing and editing the FC also attended to their own situations and concerns during the period leading to unification of the Lutheran churches and theologians of Germany in formal commitment to its final content.

My method was to look to secondary sources for references to instances in Luther's work and in the *Lutheran Confessions* that directly address the issue considered in this thesis. This was a way to manage the voluminous amount of text contained in the primary sources (Luther's publications, sermons, and lecture transcripts). I also performed electronic searches on certain key words to find further relevant references as may exist. By necessity, I had to focus in detail on certain key texts to make my arguments. I tried to enable the possibility of my own interpretation of Luther, while considering those established by other writers, but found detailed and elaborate analyses that I couldn't hope to surpass. Therefore, this thesis exhibits more the flavor of a survey tracing the development

---

5. Hamm, *Early Luther*, 60, 99, 204, 233–57.

and solidification of Lutheran interpretation during the course of the sixteenth century.

Chapter 2 examines the background and context for the emergence of Luther's teaching on justification, including his indebtedness to Augustine. Luther was an Augustinian monk before he began his career as a reformer and was of course informed by Augustine's theology, especially in the earlier years. The change in Luther's thinking is traced, in stages, but with special attention given to Luther's own description of his tower experience. The fact that Luther's own recollection is questioned by some modern scholars, together with the difficulty some have in dating Luther's change to a reformational understanding, indicates one of two things (or perhaps both). It may indicate a less-than-accurate recall by Luther of his own experience, perhaps also occasioned by a polemical necessity in promoting the doctrine later. Or, in examining Luther's writings and lectures for theological clues to the change, some modern scholars exhibit a fundamental lack of understanding as to exactly what constituted his evangelical discovery, and consequently do not identify it properly. Luther himself seems clear enough on just what that was, even if not exact on details of the circumstance. Volker Leppin, for example, argues that Luther's 1540 description of his tower experience in 1518 or 1519, is a post-facto reconstruction rather than an accurate recollection of the event. Still, it remains puzzling that Luther describes the righteousness of faith in Augustinian terms as late as 1540, since by then his theology had diverged significantly from the beloved founder of his order. None of this precludes the idea that his reformational understanding was achieved in stages, having the character of a culmination more than a singular, momentous breakthrough in the tower of Wittenberg's Black Cloister. Also open for interpretation is why Luther kept some older, medieval concepts in his theology, even as he came to vehemently oppose other medieval concepts. Everyone is a product of their times, and revolutionary thinkers are no exception. He used whatever he thought best in the project of communicating the gospel. This may be why he continued to speak of justification as ontological on occasion, even as he emphasized imputation and Paul's forensic (courtroom judgement) metaphor in other cases.

Chapter 3 describes components and resulting implications for church life and related doctrines in Luther's theology of justification. Hopefully this supplies some depth and understanding beyond terminology and changing definitions.

Chapter 4 attempts to show how Luther's thinking on the doctrine of justification emerged from his earliest medieval influences through various interlocutors along the way, including colleagues in Wittenburg as well as more ancient theologians like Anselm and most especially Augustine.

Chapter 5 discusses arguably his greatest influence of all, once the Reformation was underway, with the arrival in Wittenburg in 1518 of Philip Melanchthon.

Chapter 6 examines the framework created by the *Lutheran Confessions* for understanding justification, including the place of law in a forensic interpretation. It attempts to explain the outcome of a process of establishing a confessional identity by examining the example of the Osiandrian controversy, and its resolution in the FC.

Chapter 7 examines recent Finnish Luther studies and the impacts they may have had for good or ill. Some background is explained regarding the initiative sparked via the theological dialog between the Finnish Lutheran Church and the Russian Orthodox Church. In particular, the Eastern Orthodox doctrine of theosis is compared with the Western Church doctrine of justification. How do the fruits of this dialog further ecumenical progress and a better understanding of Luther? A key concept promoted by Tuomo Mannermaa and his associates in the Finnish Lutheran Church is that it is the indwelling Christ in the believer that justifies a person in the sight of God. This idea can find some support in Luther and other sixteenth century theologians. Dr. Kirsi Stjerna, who taught at the Lutheran Theological Seminary at Gettysburg (LTSG) and translated two of Mannermaa's most important works into English, explained that Luther did not distinguish between the person and the work of Christ. Luther spoke of receiving the whole Christ

Introduction

in faith—that he is present in faith. This would have to constitute an indwelling. It should be pointed out, however, that for Luther, such an indwelling is not a quality of merit for judgement, or a permanent possession of the believer, but rather a gift from God upon which one is totally dependent at every moment. There is also a parallel with the doctrine of the real presence of Christ in the Eucharist, a doctrine that Luther vociferously defended against all opponents in his day. The link or correlation between these general and specific modes of divine presence is something that warrants further exploration, but is beyond the immediate scope of this thesis. Chapter 7 looks at some major arguments in support of and in opposition to the Finnish perspective. Is there a perspective with qualified or partial acceptance tempered with criticism? The question of ongoing commitment in the life of the Church to historical theological formulations is also discussed, along with the need to reinterpret and improve the communication of theology as times and contexts change. For this purpose, the *Joint Declaration on the Doctrine of Justification* (JDDJ) is discussed before moving to some final conclusions. Chapter 7 also presents my conclusions based on explorations conducted in the preceding chapters. It touches on some possible consequences for ecumenical relations between different confessions of faith. The extensive work of official dialogs between different communions has taken place in the decades since Vatican II. Many topics have been studied, but for Lutherans and Roman Catholics, much effort focused on justification, as it was rightly seen as the original and primary doctrinal issue that divided Protestants from Catholics for centuries. Dr. Eric Crump, a systematics professor retired from LTSG, believes the Finnish school has made an important impact and helped create a pathway to unity among the historic Christian denominations. But is it at the expense of Lutheran identity or, for that matter, the theological identity of other denominations as well? It is true that biblical studies in the modern era have largely lost denominational characteristics. Will the same development follow with all theology? It may well be on the way to that outcome.

It is worth considering the reasons the crafters of the FC favored a forensic interpretation of justification and why they unanimously found imputation of an external righteousness such a comforting idea. I try to examine their motivations and the reasons why they are either more accurately representing Luther or are making a departure or deviation from his theology. That involves a bit of psychology and it may be that formalization of Lutheran confessional identity also involved a formalization of some aspects of Luther's psychology and personal experience. That these experiences were shared by many in the sixteenth century as Krister Stendahl has asserted,[6] would logically account for Luther's popularity in his time. Almost all of the major figures of the Reformation followed in Luther's footsteps regarding justification. This was the shared doctrine and marker of identity among Protestants, along with a rejection of papal authority. But that rejection of authority and ultimate disunity resulted from the necessity to uphold the Protestant doctrine of justification (that they thought was the very gospel) against the Roman Catholic Church's opposition to it. Therefore, justification is the true original theological reason for the Western Church's division. The related question about authority in the Church has since become primary and now dominates the discussions about overcoming divisions. Can the divisions be overcome for the sake of the unity that Jesus prayed for among his disciples? And what is the price? In the world of the twenty-first century, is it still too high, or is unity and agreement the greater necessity?

---

6. Stendahl, *Apostle Paul*, 203.

2

Background and Context for the Emergence of Luther's Theology

MARTIN LUTHER BEGAN HIS theological education and career as did other scholars of his time, studying the standard medieval primer, Peter Lombard's *Sentences*. His first preserved written "manuscript" consisted of the marginal notes he had made to his own copy. He was initially formed, like everyone else, by the medieval scholastics. But he soon came under the influence of a new and persuasive school of philosophical thought known as nominalism, spearheaded by William of Occam. The main theological exponent of this new movement was Gabiel Biel. Luther and his followers would come to oppose Biel vehemently for his synergism, though Luther did borrow from some of the nominalists' presuppositions about the nature of truth and how to discern or test it. Briefly stated, for the then-predominant old scholastic way of Thomas Aquinas and the "realists," goodness and justice were intrinsically rational by virtue of the created order. For William of Ockham, those things that are good and just are so extrinsically, simply because God declared them so. This established the philosophical foundation for the ideas of forensic justification and imputed righteousness.[1]

1. Rex, *Making of Martin Luther*, 53.

Luther was also highly influenced by Augustine while developing his understanding of justification in terms of righteousness before God. One early influence in particular came from his reading of *On the Spirit and the Letter*. Augustine's influence as well as the nominalism of Biel are discussed in more detail in chapter 4, in the context of Luther's interlocutors. One aspect is highlighted as follows because of Luther's own testimony about the turning point in his theology.

In the preface to Volume 1 of the 1545 Wittenberg edition of his Latin works, Luther described his tower experience (partly in Augustinian terms) as his breakthrough in understanding, receiving the passive righteousness of faith described by the Apostle Paul in Rom 1:17. Some scholars have disputed the notion of a sudden insight, and instead have claimed that he came to his understanding of justification in stages, culminating as he progressed as a biblical scholar, lecturer, and preacher. One such proponent is Berndt Hamm. Others have proposed specific turning points in time for his reformational breakthrough, for example Oswald Bayer or Lowell Green. That kind of specificity of course requires a definition of precisely what constituted Luther's essential and decisive theological idea against the backdrop of his time, along with documentary proof of when the idea first appeared in Luther's writings or his transcribed lectures and sermons. The dating of Luther's breakthrough realization is important because an analysis of his teaching on justification and righteousness indicates that it changes over a period of time before finally coming to rest. My argument is that the change he underwent in his thinking is how he came to a fully evangelical, reformational view that contrasted identifiably with that of the Roman Catholic Church. The accurate identification of the content of this developing reformational view depends on being able to trace the change through time. It is important also to understand the background and context for Luther's insights and development as a theologian, including his discovery of Augustine's older theology, older than the medieval scholastic theology he inherited from his own time. His influences and interlocutors are treated in greater detail in chapters 4 and 5.

Background and Context

LUTHER'S OWN ACCOUNT: THE "TOWER EXPERIENCE"

It is so named because it reputedly took place in Luther's study room in the tower of the Black Cloister Monastery in Wittenberg where he lived as a monk. The exact date of Luther's experience here is uncertain, but very likely early in 1519 by Luther's own account, approximately coinciding with his second series of lectures on the *Psalms* during the 1518–19 school year. The key item in this recounting is Luther's change in understanding of justifying grace as passive rather than active from the perspective of the person who hears the gospel in faith. Prior to this, even up through his exposition of the theology of the cross in the Heidelberg Disputation, Luther thought that justification depended on humility (nearly equated with faith; and with pride being the chief sin) before God,[2] and this was consonant with the standard Catholic teaching that the human being must actively and willfully cooperate with grace for justification. If a person affirms God's judgment on sin, then God could justify the sinner. With the tower experience, he formed the opinion that God alone is active in justification.

Luther had struggled with the interpretation of Rom 1:17 earlier in his lectures of 1515–16. Taking his cue from Augustine's *On the Spirit and the Letter*, he said this: "Therefore it is called the righteousness of God because he makes them just by imparting it. For example, health is of the Lord, by which he makes them healthy."[3] In these lectures Luther had taught that not works of the law but rather works of faith proceeding from infused grace by the Holy Spirit brought about justification. Luther had the insight from Augustine (and that went back even further in Catholic theology) that the righteousness of God was the cause of salvation rather than simply punitive judgement, but still maintained with him that it was imparted through inner renewal. Later, by his own recollection, Luther had the further insight that justification did not depend on righteousness within a person, but on what he

---

2. *Luther's Works*, American Edition (LW) 31:47 (Ch 3.4.8).
3. LW 25:151.

liked to call the "alien" or extrinsic righteousness of Christ, given to the sinner as a gift through faith. Here (in 1545) he recalls that experience:

> Meanwhile... I hated that word "righteousness of God," which, according to the use and custom of all the teachers, I had been taught to understand philosophically regarding the formal or active righteousness, as they called it, with which God is righteous and punishes the unrighteous sinner... I felt that I was a sinner before God with an extremely disturbed conscience. I could not believe that he was placated by my satisfaction. I did not love, yes, I hated the righteous God who punishes sinners, and secretly, if not blasphemously, certainly murmuring greatly, I was angry with God... At last, by the mercy of God, meditating day and night, I gave heed to the context of the words, namely, "In it the righteousness of God is revealed, as it is written, 'He who through faith is righteous shall live.'" There I began to understand that the righteousness of God is that by which the righteous lives by a gift of God, namely by faith... the passive righteousness with which merciful God justifies us by faith, as it is written, "He who through faith is righteous shall live." Here I felt that I was altogether born again and had entered paradise itself through open gates... And I extolled my sweetest word with a love as great as the hatred with which I had before hated the word "righteousness of God."... Later I read Augustine's *The Spirit and the Letter*, where contrary to hope I found that he, too, interpreted God's righteousness in a similar way, as the righteousness with which God clothes us when he justifies us. Although this was heretofore said imperfectly and he did not explain all things concerning imputation clearly, it nevertheless was pleasing that God's righteousness with which we are justified was taught.[4]

Why was this experience so meaningful and powerful for Luther? This is described further in a subsequent paragraph on the promise and faith in it, and his release from anfechtung. Luther's

---

4. LW 34:336–37.

spiritual struggle throughout the previous period up through 1518 was to find an entirely gracious God and certainty of salvation. If salvation was granted for the righteousness within a person, one could never be sure whether one's faith was adequate, or if one's works of faith, even if wrought by the Holy Spirit, were enough. Acceptance by God was contingent upon spiritual attainment. After his breakthrough, Luther changed his heretofore Catholic view and instead emphatically affirmed the certainty of salvation obtained via faith. He also, while praising Augustine for helping him get partway there, differentiated himself by associating his discovering of passive alien righteousness with Christ's righteousness imputed rather than (completely) infused in the believer. In this matter he found ultimately that Augustine hadn't fully understood Paul or explained the doctrine adequately.

LUTHER'S OWN ACCOUNT: LAW AND GOSPEL

Luther himself spoke alternatively of the breakthrough in his thinking, when he learned to distinguish law and gospel. In one of his Table Talks (no. 5518, informal comments transcribed by one of his students, Caspar Heydenreich, in the winter of 1542–43), he says this:

> For a long time, I went astray [in the monastery] and didn't know what I was about . . . To be sure, I knew something, but I didn't know what it was until I came to the text in *Romans* 1 [:17], "He who through faith is righteous shall live." I learned to distinguish between the righteousness of the law and the righteousness of the gospel. I lacked nothing before this except that I made no distinction between the law and the gospel . . . But when I discovered the proper distinction—namely, that the law is one thing and the gospel is another—I made myself free.[5]

Luther regarded making this distinction the mark of a true theologian, correctly dividing the Word of truth, as Paul

---

5. LW 54:442–43.

admonishes Timothy (2 Tim 2:15). This was the proper way to consider all topics in theology and biblical interpretation. In his treatise *On the Freedom of a Christian*, Luther explains how he regarded faith alone (apart from works) as that which makes one righteous before God. The scriptures contain commands from God (law) about doing good works but these don't actually thereby happen, because they don't empower a person to obey them. According to Luther, they are instead made to show a person's inability to fulfill them and cause one to despair so as to seek help elsewhere from someone else, namely Christ (the second use of the law).

This despair entails fear of the wrath of God and damnation for not fulfilling the commands. Following this (penultimate) Word of the law, there follows the ultimate Word of the gospel. These are the promises or assurances, that if believed, do fulfill all commands and requirements from God. The promises bring "all grace, righteousness, peace, and freedom." If the promises are not believed, one has nothing, and the law simply leads to death. Even further, Luther casts faith as having the power to free a person from evil desires and sins. In conclusion, everything is from God—the commandments, and their fulfillment in Christ.[6]

THE PROMISE COMMUNICATED FROM GOD AS THE GOSPEL

According to Oswald Bayer's analysis,[7] the promise of God to forgive and reconcile the sinner to himself in Christ, and thereby make the sinner righteous in God's sight, constituting the power of the gospel to save, is the genuine turning point driving the reformational, evangelical impulse in Luther's theology. It is this point in Luther's experience that came to serve as the normative function of theology for the churches that bear his name, and is in fact responsible for the existence of Protestant churches. Several things that marked Luther's theology and that of the Lutheran churches

---

6. LW 31:348–49; LW 36:48.
7. Bayer, *Martin Luther's Theology*, 44.

follow closely but secondarily from this turning point, most especially in distinguishing the gospel from the law (both of which come as a self-communication from God). Formulations of how justification takes place (by faith alone) and Luther's descriptions of two kinds of righteousness (active and passive) are also logical consequences from interpretating scripture in light of this driving impulse.

PROMISE AND FAITH

According to Bayer, the text from Luther that is most definitive about the reformational turning point is found in his treatise *On the Babylonian Captivity of the Church*[8] because it clearly sets forth the relationship between promise and faith in a way unmatched in previous publications, and that was used in a consistent way in Luther's writings thereafter. This is a persuasive argument from the historiographical point of view, but it documents a turning point that should properly be considered the initiation of a series of further developments that take place gradually over the next several years toward his stable, fully reformational theology. It was there "articulated in a very specific verbal way, set within a very critical time in history that involved systematic questions and theological controversies . . . this treatise caused a sharply negative reaction from the Roman Catholic Church that . . . resulted in the most important decrees made at the Council of Trent. These included definitions concerning how the sacraments are to be understood, the scholastic definition of justification, and the most negative reaction of all, the statement concerning this treatise and its impacts."[9]

Luther saw God's promise of salvation as communicated through preaching of the Word and administration of the sacraments: first, in baptism, and then through a return to the effects of baptism in the Lord's Supper, its purpose highlighted in the words of institution, "Take; eat; this is my body which is given for you . . .

---

8. LW 36:38–52, 56–62; 64–67, 82–85, 123–24.
9. Bayer, *Martin Luther's Theology,* 45–46.

Drink of it, all of you. This cup is the New Testament in my blood, shed for you for the forgiveness of sins." (Lutheran liturgy)[10]

The Word in this case, the promise, brings about what it says, as a performative speech-act that communicates and effectively establishes a new relationship in reality.[11] Luther says, "The blessing in actuality is truly divine; for when God blesses, the result is the thing itself or that which is said, in accordance with those well-known statements: 'For He commanded, and they were created' (Ps 148:5) and 'God said: Let there be light; and there was light' (Gen 1:3). He is One who blesses with effect and does all things through what He says, because His Word is the thing itself, and His blessing is an abundant blessing, physically as well as spiritually."[12]

The earliest appearance of this promisio in Luther's writing occurs in the summer of 1518, in his fifty theses of the disputation *For the Investigation of Truth and for the Comfort of Troubled Consciences*. The term "righteousness of God" from Rom 1:17 cited in Luther's 1545 explication of his tower experience could function as a summary of these theses in discussing the sacrament of penance, representing a point of convergence between that explication and reflections in his lectures on Genesis, also from 1545. Luther's own claims about the dating of his evangelical breakthrough have been questioned as perhaps a product of faltering memory in old age, or as projection backward in time to justify his position in conflicts with the religious authorities. His recollection of the tower experience in the 1545 preface to his collected Latin works is an authentic primary source and shouldn't be discounted. In it, he says that he hadn't understood the gospel until the 1518–19 school year, when he had taken up a second cycle of interpreting and lecturing on the *Psalms*.

The term "righteousness of God" has its roots in scripture and in the Augustinian tradition. It is also mentioned in the decrees of the Council of Trent, many of which were formulated in direct opposition to the Reformation. According to Oswald Bayer, the

10. *Evangelical Lutheran Worship*, 108.
11. LW 5:140.
12. LW 4:154–55.

theses of this disputation in 1518 represent the first reformational text because it provides an articulation of the assurance of salvation, which was Luther's chief concern. It was this that was "the decisive point of contention between Luther and representatives of the Roman Catholic Church—which reached a high point in the hearing in Augsburg before Cardinal Cajetan in October 1518."[13] Luther contended that believing the promise and having that assurance was what made one a Christian. He also characterizes it as a surprising new discovery that he had made, the promise "shining forth once again, though it was obscure and unknown to all the theologians throughout the papacy."[14]

ANFECHTUNG AND THE INTROSPECTIVE CONSCIENCE

Luther was concerned above all to find certainty of salvation. I focus in this section on Luther's spiritual and emotional struggle, and argue that this overriding concern and necessity applied to very many others during his time, which is why it resonated so strongly. This is what ultimately lead to his theological breakthrough and the Reformation. This also extends down to our time, beyond even Paul's framework when discussing justification in his time. Certainty was not offered by the medieval church of Luther's time—only the hope of God's favorable disposition at the final judgement, if one had become worthy through following the Church's prescriptions, especially partaking of the sacraments. Saving faith for him was faith in this promise from God, in the face of what one inevitably observes when looking at oneself in the "mirror" of the law. He arrived at this conception through a prolonged personal struggle with his conscience, as is well-known. Luther keenly felt anfechtung, a German word meaning "all the doubt, turmoil, pangs, tremor, panic, despair, desolation, and desperation

---

13. Bayer, *Martin Luther's Theology*, 50.
14. LW 8:192.

which invade the weight of man."[15] Of course, an exhortation to faith was included in those prescriptions. But for Luther, faith was the all-consuming and only necessity, something to cling to as the antidote to anfechtung (which could be seen variously as a trial from God, the wrath of God experienced through the law, or an assault by the Devil). Theses fifteen and sixteen of his ninety-five are reproduced below.

> 15. This fear or horror is sufficient in itself, to say nothing of other things, to constitute the penalty of purgatory, since it is very near the horror of despair.
> 16. Hell, purgatory, and heaven seem to differ the same as despair, fear, and assurance of salvation.[16]

Luther dwelt with images of suffering and guilt as if in continual prayer and groaning, as illustrated by the following excerpts from his *Explanations of* the *Ninety-Five Theses* published nearly a year later, in August 1518. They most vividly describe his feelings of anfechtung:

> They were so great and so much like hell that no tongue could adequately express them, no pen could describe them, and one who had not himself experienced them could not believe them. And so great were they that, if they had been sustained or had lasted for half an hour, even for one tenth of an hour, he would have perished completely and all of his bones would have been reduced to ashes . . . In this instance the person is stretched out with Christ so that all his bones may be counted, and every corner of the soul is filled with the greatest bitterness, dread, trembling, and sorrow in such a manner that all these last forever . . . the soul, at the point where it is touched by a passing eternal flood, feels and imbibes nothing except eternal punishment . . . if that punishment of hell, that is, that unbearable and inconsolable trembling, takes hold of the living, punishment of the souls in purgatory seems to be so much greater.[17]

15. Bainton, *Here I Stand*, 42.
16. LW 31:29.
17. LW 31:129–30.

Nowadays, few if any people experience the intensity of Luther's anfechtung, so we don't really accept it as some kind of norm or necessity for faith. But in his time, it resonated with many. Krister Stendahl makes this point in his essay about what he calls the introspective conscience of the West.[18] He presents a convincing case that feelings of guilt or a personal burden of conscience were not Paul's concerns related to justification in his authentic New Testament letters. Rather, justification was primarily about the issue of fellowship between the Jews and Gentiles. If this is a correct reading of Paul, he apparently took for granted the justification (in the sense of salvation) of both groups, especially the people to whom he was writing. In other words, he wasn't struggling with, or trying to convince people about their standing with God, or ease their consciences. The more modern issue in Luther's time and beyond definitely foregrounded those very concerns. But Stendahl, arguing this case before the committee tasked with forming the Evangelical Lutheran Church in America (ELCA), maintained that justification was not the central concern of Paul, or of the New Testament. Some members of the committee disagreed strongly and controversies among theologians have been ongoing over this question.

Paul had a robust conscience with regard to his fulfilment of the law, but nevertheless had come to see it as "refuse" in light of his vision on the road to Damascus and his conversion to faith in Jesus as the Messiah. This new path of salvation was open to both Jews and Gentiles, and no longer required conformance to the law for justification, which had been the line of demarcation and religious identity between them as far as Paul was concerned (Phil 3:5–9).[19]

By the time of Augustine, Jewish-Gentile relations were no longer a live theological concern. The shift to heavy subjective introspection was first found in a major way in Christian literature with Augustine's *Confessions*. In Augustine's conflict against the Donatists, he argued that "The Catholic Church was a church not

---

18. Stendahl, *Apostle Paul*, 199–215.
19. Stendahl, *Apostle Paul*, 200–201.

so much of the pure as those who tried or longed to be pure."[20] Accordingly, for Augustine, the primary moral criteria for justification before God was rightness of intention, that is, motivation by properly directed love. Virtuous love was to be directed toward God, rather than self or created things. Created things were good but not ends in themselves. One should love things only insofar as they helped one to connect with God. As a result, as can be seen in his *Confessions*, a constant introspection was necessary for a person to ascertain and evaluate the rightness of their motivations and the quality of their love.[21] After Christian missions to Europe had established a new Christian culture and tradition, "the theological and practical center of penance shifted from baptism, administered once and for all, to the ever-repeated Mass," which contributed to an even more acute introspection in the Christian life.[22]

THE MEDIEVAL PENITENTIAL SYSTEM

Martin Luther was a thoroughly Augustinian monk. The Augustinian line of thought leads into the Middle Ages and reaches its climax in Luther's penitential struggle and his interpretation of Paul.[23] It is evident that Luther's thinking proceeded at first from a profound spiritual discomfort with what was then the contemporary practice of penance and indulgences. In Catholic theology two things were involved in the sacrament of penance. The guilt of sin was removed by forgiveness, while the penalty of sin was removed by the believer doing acts of penance.[24] Luther's initial concern, expressed in the *Ninety-Five Theses*, was that the penitential system was leading to a kind of moral hazard and laxity in the Church and a potential false sense of security on the part of penitents. The literal meaning of the word "indulge" suggests

20. MacCulloch, *Christianity*, 304.
21. Tornau, "Augustine of Hippo," para. 7.3.
22. Stendahl, *Apostle Paul*, 203.
23. Stendahl, *Apostle Paul*, 206.
24. Green, *How Melanchthon Helped Luther*, 78.

this. Hence, in thesis forty he proposes: "A Christian who is truly contrite seeks and loves to pay penalties for his sins; the bounty of indulgences, however, relaxes penalties and causes men to hate them—at least it furnishes occasion for hating them."[25] Luther had set the entire tone for the theses with the first one: "When our Lord and Master Jesus Christ said, 'Repent' [Matt 4:17], he willed the entire life of believers to be one of repentance."[26] The kind of self-examination required for good confession and performance of penance didn't give Luther peace. Within a half-year Luther reversed this underlying attitude 180 degrees by claiming utterly free grace and forgiveness of sin on account of faith alone. Though indulgences in theory remitted only temporal penalties rather than provide forgiveness of sin as such, it seemed as though God were offering a plenary indulgence for past, present, and future sin without requiring any effort, punishment, or expense whatsoever.

What Luther was after was certain assurance of salvation, which he associated both with forgiveness of sin and as a remedy for the sinful nature he experienced within himself. He found that assurance while interpreting Paul. Paul, though, had nothing to say about forgiveness of personal sin or shortcomings in his undisputed epistles. There is the notable instance of calling himself "the chief of sinners" for his previous persecution of Christians. Even then he didn't dwell on it, and used it as a before-and-after illustration of how he was now pressing forward with his new mission, "forgetting what lies behind" (Phil 3:13).

The fact that Luther found his remedy for a tormented conscience in biblical passages that to him meant something different than what Paul had in mind, doesn't negate Luther's interpretation, but it presented a challenge to conclusions drawn from the debate Luther had with Rome. Several years ago, I called in to a religious talk show broadcasting on a local AM radio station (part of the conservative Roman Catholic EWTN global radio network). They were inviting Protestants to call in to discuss why they were Protestants, ostensibly to persuade them otherwise. I called in and we

---

25. LW 31:29.
26. LW 31:23.

briefly discussed "justification by faith alone." Interestingly, they cited modern studies by the "new perspective on Paul" advocates like Stendahl and others to demonstrate that Luther had simply been incorrect in his interpretation. I was surprised, as I hadn't expected historical criticism to be approved by the hosts on this traditionalist radio program.

The historical context was much different, and Luther seemingly read his concerns back in time into the first century. Today this might be attributed to a type of common exegetical error called contemporaneity, exhibited by many interpreters. However, in this case it is not simply an error to be dismissed. For his part, at the conclusion of his essay *The Apostle Paul and the Introspective Conscience of the West*, Stendahl did not completely dismiss Luther or his insights. His was a pioneering breakthrough in theology. It addressed the great spiritual need of the sixteenth century and beyond. Given the burden of introspective consciences, the threat of sudden death from the Black Plague, and the penitential system that had developed in the Church, Luther and others wanted desperately to find a gracious God. At that time, it was taught that if a person died without having properly confessed sin, they would face eternal damnation. The gospel needed to be applied to the more general, universal, and timeless human predicament of sin, beyond what Paul had considered, to a deeper psychological layer of thought.[27] This would have been congruent with Augustine and others' view that texts of scripture could have or support multiple meanings.

Ironically, Luther rejected the medieval scholastic four-fold approach to interpretation, especially the allegorical, contending instead that there was one true meaning for any particular biblical text—the one intended by the Holy Spirit. He insisted on beginning with the plain meaning of the words themselves, otherwise interpretations could become too fanciful, unmoored from reality. As he went on in his studies and theological battles, he became confident (some say arrogant and egotistical) that his interpretation was the correct one, from God, against all opponents. Theologians

27. Stendahl, *Apostle Paul*, 204–5.

and ecumenists today will appreciate Luther's insights and how they have shaped Western thought, while putting them into context along with others, perhaps including new ones stimulated by historical studies that echo the Reformation slogan of "back to the sources."

3

Components in Luther's Theology of Justification

THE PREVIOUS CHAPTER DESCRIBED the background and context for the emergence of Luther as pioneer of the Reformation. It also proposed a primary turning point and important closely related concepts framing his theology of justification. The identification of a turning point was based on his own account later (remembrance) and on a historical analysis of his first consistent and definitive departure from what was considered orthodox Catholic theology of the time. In this chapter I discuss those basic components that were identifiably constitutive, so as to show Luther's progression and the resulting implications of the early Reformation for Christian faith. Bernt Hamm, for example, tries to take a somewhat different approach than those who have sought to precisely pinpoint a definitive turn. In contrast he wishes to show re-orientation in stages, piecing them together into a whole picture that shows how critical Reformation ideas marked a new understanding of Christian faith—how it differed from the traditional Catholic understanding from which it emerged in the late Middle Ages. It is problematic, however, to map the development in Luther's theology in a clear chronological manner, and Hamm does not do this directly. Rather, the stages are presented thematically in his work, although dates of related milestones are sometimes referenced. Primarily, Luther moved along as he felt compelled to respond to: specific problems; controversies that were pressed upon him; contemporary events; the needs of pastoral care; and conflicts, reactions, and challenges brought about by his preaching, teaching, and publishing. He did move toward an extrinsic, passive characterization of justification, although he retained a sanative aspect in some of his writings, depending on the contexts of his explanations, especially earlier in his career. For example, this occurs in his lectures on *Romans*. He had made an allegorical interpretation of the *Parable of the Good Samaritan*. He later referenced this explanation again in 1521 in his treatise *Against Latomas*.[1] By 1522, however, he had made a distinction between justification and sanctification, with sanctification following, in a similar way that good works follow as the fruit of faith.

In terms of a general time frame, a big change began in the Spring of 1518, in the aftermath of the indulgence controversy. According to Richard Rex, in late 1517, after the *Ninety-Five Theses* had been completed and sent to Albrecht, the Archbishop of Mainz, Luther was still working conceptually within Catholic orthodoxy and its penitential system.[2] That quickly changed, spurred on by reactions to him. As I explained in the previous chapter, Oswald Bayer also dates the definitive change to the same general time in 1518. A myriad of others identified Luther's early commentary on *Galatians* as the definitive point in his view of justification. It was planned at the end of 1518 as a more developed exposition of the theology emergent from his lectures on Paul's letter during the previous two years. It was written from February to May and printed widely in 1519.

The motif of God's promise of forgiveness with unconditional acceptance for Christ's sake, and a sinner's faith in that promise, brought with it immediate certainty of salvation. This claim emerged as the initial reformational idea about effective righteousness before God, and was contrary to Catholic tradition. In that

1. LW 32:232.
2. Rex, *Making of Martin Luther*, 14.

tradition, there could be no certainty (which was considered presumptuous), only hope.

Also in Rex's estimation, by 1525 Luther had essentially finished his creative innovative phase, and had arrived at fixed theological positions.[3] According to Rex, Luther's view of justification was shaped by the medieval scholastic indulgence theory it opposed, and was mature before 1520. And, according to Berndt Hamm, all the decisive components of the Reformation can be found in Luther's early publications prior to his appearance to defend himself at the Diet of Worms in 1521.[4] He defines the period before that as "early Luther." Luther moved forward from that point to apply his new theology to reforming the contemporary situation and practice in the Church. What we have then, is a frenetic period of activity and theological development in the space of three years from 1518 to 1521 that had a dramatic and lasting historical impact on Christianity. It was a radical redefinition of faith and how it operated in the life of the believer.

Berndt Hamm lists nine important teachings of Luther that in his estimation are decisive components of his theology regarding justification.[5] These came to be established as Luther emerged and diverged from the traditional Catholic religious system he inherited. They were also evident as starting points influencing other streams of the Reformation (besides Lutheranism), albeit with some differences in direction. In the following subparagraphs each of these is elaborated.

AUTHORITATIVE BASIS

Luther came to the conclusion that if the papacy opposed the gospel (as he and his followers understood it), a change in the locus of authority was needed. He located that authority in the Christian scriptures alone, and they became the supporting

---

3. Rex, *Making of Martin Luther*, 208.
4. Hamm, *Early Luther*, 255.
5. Hamm, *Early Luther*, 256–57.

absolute certainty of truth for the absolute certainty of salvation via justifying faith.

The Catholic argument against Sola Scriptura employed Augustine's famous statement that he would not believe in the gospel unless the authority of the Church caused him to do so. Luther recalled that Dr. Usinger, a theology teacher at Erfurt, warned him against using the Bible directly as authoritative because doing so gave rise to factions. Usinger recommended instead the ancient doctors of the Church, who he said had properly distilled the truth out of the Bible.[6]

Luther distinguished and ranked books and portions of the Bible in terms of relative clarity, value, and usefulness regarding communication of the gospel. As is well-known, he thought *James* to be poor enough that it should be excluded from the canon. He believed James was not genuinely apostolic because it explicitly contradicted Paul on the doctrine of justification apart from works. Philip Melanchthon made a very clever attempt at harmonizing the two by analyzing and interpreting James' words very closely. According to him, Paul was referring to justification before God, while James was referring to justification before men when he talked about showing his faith by his works (Jas 2:18). In 1533 (in the Table Talk collected by Conrad Cordatus), Luther said he hadn't been convinced by Melanchthon's belabored argument in the *Apology of the Augsburg Confession*, preferring instead to view the words of James in a simple straightforward manner.[7]

DIRECT ACCESS AND RECEPTION

Christians receive the mercy of God directly through faith, independent of Church authority or mediation by Mary and the saints. This idea was the first step toward a heightened focus on the individual in Protestant theologies of salvation. Luther regarded the Mass as a testament or promise rather than a propitiatory sacrifice

---

6. LW 54:128.
7. Kolb and Wengert, *Book of Concord*, 157–59.

on the part of either the gathered congregation with its presiding priest, or in the case of votive Masses, the priest alone offering the Mass. This effectively undermined the forms of intercession offered by the sacred office of the Church. "The Mass is a divine promise, that can benefit no one, be applied to no one, intercede for no one, and be communicated to no one, except only to him who believes with a faith of his own. Who can receive or apply, in behalf of another, the promise of God, which demands the personal faith of each one individually?"[8] However, Luther did extol the communion of saints as providing a sheltering grace in death, in association with Christ and his promise.[9]

FORGIVENESS OF SIN AND ETERNAL LIFE

This is received by all Christians through justifying faith, which is seen as the chief article in the Christian faith. Luther famously called it the article by which the Church stands or falls. How does forgiveness happen from the point of view of the Divine, according to him? Luther sometimes used language of the substitutionary atonement theory derived from Anselm, but importantly, he also highlighted the classic "Christus Victor" motif that came from early church fathers and had its origin in the New Testament. This viewpoint can clearly be seen in his famous hymn, *A Mighty Fortress*. There is victory over sin, death, and the devil (or hell) for our redemption by the blood and innocent suffering and death of Jesus Christ, according to the explanation of the second article of the *Apostle's Creed* in Luther's *Small Catechism*.[10] It can also be characterized as God's action to reconcile with the world.

In 1531 in one of his Table Talks, Luther stated that he regarded his theology of 1519, the year of his shorter commentary on *Galatians*, as weak in comparison to his later work. He had gained some insight toward a reformational stance, but was essentially still

---

8. LW 36:48.
9. Hamm, *Early Luther*, 150.
10. Kolb and Wengert, *Book of Concord*, 355.

Catholic in his thinking.[11] In chapter 6, I make a further comparison of the main difference between his shorter and longer *Galatians* commentaries regarding justification and righteousness. But for the present discussion about atonement theories, in Luther's longer commentary on *Galatians* (1535), he states that the curse, or the wrath of God against the world (sin), was in conflict with the blessing of God's eternal grace and mercy. This points to a duality of law and gospel, which Luther himself claims was the key to his breakthrough in understanding. The curse had to yield to the divine eternal blessing in Christ.[12] He goes on to say that our faith is our victory (from the Gospel of John) and that this is the primary Christian teaching. This sharply dualistic characterization of God connects the Atonement with the Incarnation, and hence the necessity of confessing Christ's divinity, for that is what ensured the victory of the blessing. In his book about the main historical atonement theories, Gustav Aulén commented on these ideas and Luther's very sharp and striking dualism. "But though the wrath of God is identical with his will, yet it is, according to Luther, a 'tyrant' in that is opposed to the Divine Love . . . it would seem almost that the conflict were carried back within the Divine being itself . . . yet it is the blessing that represents His inmost nature."[13] Aulén also says some other things concerning justification in his systematic theology. He favors the Christus Victor motif over Anselm's substitutionary atonement theory and characterizes forensic justification as "legalistic." He argues that reconciliation with God is personal and involves more than simply acquittal and remission of punishment under the law. This points to the sense that a single metaphor, although Pauline (such as a courtroom scene to illustrate an atonement theory) is not adequate by itself to fully describe God's gracious action in Christ.[14] That being said, it does fit well with a clear distinction between law and gospel, which Luther described as his breakthrough in theology and that he considered normative.

11. Green, *How Melanchthon Helped Luther*, 68.
12. LW 26:281–82.
13. Aulén, *Christus Victor*, 114.
14. Aulén, *Faith of the Christian Church*, 265–66.

UNCONDITIONAL GRACE AND SALVATION

With the grace of God being unconditional, Christians are divinely adopted as children and become heirs of salvation. Having received forgiveness of sin won by Christ and operating solely through faith, as described in the previous paragraph, they are free from all guilt and penalties, including the temporal ones that were thought to be mitigated by indulgences. This marked a change from the medieval centering of salvation around the necessity of a contrite heart—a sorrowful love of God exhibited in true repentance, especially before death.[15] In both Catholic and Protestant theology, justification is purely by the grace of God (Sola Gratia). But in Catholic theology that grace is described as something that is poured into the soul (infused) and enables a person to love God wholly, if the person cooperates. In scholastic theology, infused grace comes through the operation of the sacraments, especially confession and communion. They conferred grace on those who were predisposed to receive them properly and thereby benefit.[16] Augustine spoke of love properly directed—toward God rather than created things, as the important factor. This love of God is rewarded by progressively more grace (therein lies the conditionality), and ultimately with salvation. Judgement happens at death, and depends on whether one had a truly repentant heart and cooperated in a worthy manner with God's grace.

INDEPENDENT OF RENEWAL (THE ORDER OF SALVATION)

Salvation is for the sake of Christ alone, not by any internal spiritual quality or by any action on the part of the believer. No performance of external good works affects one's right standing with God. God alone, through the work of Christ, accomplishes salvation that effects renewal and transformation. The renewal does not result in salvation but rather results from it.

15. Hamm, *Early Luther*, 8.
16. Rex, *Making of Martin Luther*, 74.

PERSONAL CERTAINTY

If salvation is unconditional and independent of the worthiness of a person to receive it, that makes it possible to be certain of it, contrary to what was taught by the Roman Catholic Church. In the medieval church, consistent with Augustine, it was taught that justification was a life process, propelled by the grace of God. Salvation occurred after death at final judgement. In life, grace enabled a person to remove sin, become sanctified, practice love, fulfill the law, and become worthy of salvation. This process of justification (functionally equivalent to sanctification) involved a moral transformation that enabled a person to love God.[17] That was the highest virtue in the Catholic Church. From the Apostle Paul's conclusion to his famous exposition on the gift of love: "And now faith, hope, and love remain, these three. And the greatest of these is love." (1 Cor 13:13). The Catholic Church calls these the three theological virtues. Love ranks higher even than faith, which was the critical factor in justification according to the reformers. For them, faith meant complete instant justification and salvation as an event here and now (rather than a current process and future verdict).

Certainty of salvation is of the very essence of faith according to Luther, because faith is trusting in God's love and that what God promises is true. A faithful individual will inevitably acknowledge his or her unworthiness (looking at the sinful self) but nevertheless trust God's declaration of righteousness as provided in Christ. The humility of acknowledging one's unworthiness is a necessary aspect of saving faith.

GOOD WORKS AS FRUITS

Love is indeed a high virtue, but always imperfect in human beings. The human manifestation of love as the greatest virtue described by Paul is an idealistic portrait of what it should be. Only Christ manifested that love perfectly and it could only be appropriated

17. Hamm, *Early Luther*, 238.

by the rest of us through faith in him. That being said, early on, Luther did describe faith, hope, and love as a unified whole, with love assimilated into faith. From his first lectures/commentary (1513–5) on the *Psalms* (119:162): "For this reason we rejoice, because we believe the divine promises, and we hope for and love the things he promises."[18] In many lectures and commentaries, Luther is keen to emphasize that genuine faith is active in love, and necessarily produces good works. Faith always comes first and drives love. One could say that faith forms love rather than speaking of "faith formed by love," which was a common expression used by medieval theologians. Later, in his 1535 commentary on *Galatians* (chapters 2 and 3), Luther objects to this phrase several times, believing that faith is primary and that human love even though it may be motivated by God, is a response, and remains imperfect in this life. Faith however, doesn't have this transitory or incomplete quality, but instead justifies perfectly. He uses Paul's assertions about faith justifying apart from works to refute the arguments about faith formed by love, reasoning that the phrase is only a more sophisticated way of claiming that works justify, precisely because love in action equals good works.[19]

Works performed freely out of love for God and neighbor follow naturally from having a living faith. They are not conditions to be satisfied or merits offered to God. In the late Middle Ages good works in the context of the penitential system had become associated with satisfaction of temporal penalties for sin. This was a shift in direction from an earlier emphasis on purification.[20] Good works were often specified by a priest in confession as penitential acts to demonstrate sincerity of repentance.

18. LW 11:518.
19. LW 26:136–37; LW 27:28, 64.
20. Hamm, *Early Luther*, 12.

Components in Luther's Theology of Justification

TRADITIONAL ATTEMPTS TO ACTIVELY REACH SALVATION ARE OBSOLETE

This includes things such as calling upon saints, funding charities or private Masses, buying indulgences, and following prescribed prayers, procedures, and established protocols to prepare for "a good death." Finally, after death, one willingly accepted the punishments and purification of purgatory, in preparation for heaven. These were all common medieval practices and concerns, even if not all of them were entirely prescribed by official Church teaching.

According to various texts about the *Ars Moriendi* (*Art of Dying*), composed in the context of the Black Plague in Europe, temptations thought to be acute and especially to be avoided at death included lack of faith, despair, impatience, spiritual pride, and avarice. There were also great uncertainties involved: the time and manner, one's state of grace, and the result of the judgement.[21] What was needed at the hour of death were true repentance, humility, piety, and hopefulness. The purpose of the *Ars Moriendi* was to keep death and preparation for it vivid in the minds of the living, so that one was motivated to live a worthy and pious life of humility and repentance. This was entirely congruent with Luther's viewpoint as late as the printing of his *Ninety-Five Theses* (October 1517), the first of which stated: "When our Lord and Master Jesus Christ said, 'Repent' [Matt 4:17], he willed the entire life of believers to be one of repentance."[22] Salutary as this admonition may be, for a culture fixated on (often unexpected) death and safe passage to a blissful eternity, the effect was to focus people on their inner piety, humility, and lifelong spiritual preparation in cooperation with God's grace, as the proper way of salvation. Lest this be labeled a subtle form of works-righteousness, it should be noted that the focus was on attitudes of trust and devotion toward God rather than a person's outward actions.[23] This seems close to (the inward aspect of) Reformation faith, and is perhaps why Luther chose to write about it.

---

21. Hamm, *Early Luther*, 118.
22. LW 31:25.
23. Hamm, *Early Luther*, 123.

Following in the tradition of *Ars Moriendi*, Luther wrote his *Sermon on Preparing to Die* in October 1519, for the purpose of helping people to die confidently in Christ.[24] It was the first Reformation writing on the subject, and enjoyed wide circulation and popularity. It was composed with spiritual comfort for the individual layperson in mind as its primary concern. The traditional literature on this topic served to remind readers of the nearness of death and its occasion for the moment of individual judgement. Of course, this had special terrifying resonance during the time of the plague. It also had great resonance with Luther due to his unusually intense experience of anfechtung, as described in the previous chapter. While it is hardly typical for most modern believers, this sermon and his attitude toward anfechtung indicates how Luther in his time considered his spiritual experience in this regard as normative for Christian faith. As illustrated in this sermon, and in his 1524 revision of the hymn *In the Midst of Life We Are*[25] regarding the time of death, Luther expressed traditionally the twin aspects of the fear experienced in anfechtung and the comfort of the gospel in salvation, particularly with faith in the promise given in the sacrament and the declaration of absolution.[26] Both the promise and the declaration are God's Word to the recipient, and are to be regarded therefore as absolutely and unconditionally true.

What, then, put an effective end to the *Ars Moriendi* in the Reformation? It was the new view of justification—no longer dependent on notions of cooperation with grace, satisfaction for sin (personal atonement), merit, or a cultivated perfection of interior virtues that reached a climax at the point of death. Luther's shift in perspective was from internal self-examination to an identity one finds externally, as evidenced in his 1519 *Sermon on Preparing to Die*: "Seek yourself only in Christ and not in yourself and you will find yourself in him eternally."[27]

---

24. LW 42:100–15.
25. LW 53:276.
26. LW 42:110.
27. LW 42:106.

No longer thought of as simply a beginning that sets in motion the process of sanctification, justification is a proleptic final verdict, a salvation granted immediately in the midst of life (here and now) that carries on through death (but is not focused upon it). It removes the anxiety associated with death. Hearing the gospel, fear of hell is replaced by joyful certainty, both in life and death. "To the extent that a Christian believes, to that extent he is in heaven."[28] Luther showed that he regarded heaven, hell, and purgatory as existential spiritual states, rather than physical places. Since God has already dismissed all punishment for the faithful, the notion of purgatory disappeared from Protestant teaching, along with indulgences and their use in fundraising for the Church.

REPENTANCE AS SIGN OF FREE (GIFTED) SALVATION

In the Reformation understanding of justification as an event in the here and now, simple observation confirms that sin remains in Christians, that is, in those who have been justified. In this view, believers are simultaneously sinners and justified before God. Thesis one of Luther's famous ninety-five thereby took on a somewhat different meaning from medieval Catholicism, but there was also continuity with it in the sense that contrition or sorrow for sin resulted from the love of God and his righteousness. The entire life of believers is still to be one of repentance, but not to gain forgiveness or favor. Rather it is lived out of gratefulness and thankfulness, with the desire to do right out of love for God, who already shows grace and favor before any repentance. As such, repentance is a sign of the justification that has already occurred.

---

28. LW 26:440.

4

Influences, Interlocuters, and Developments

THE PREVIOUS CHAPTER DESCRIBED basic essential components of Luther's theology of justification that are identifiably constitutive of a reformational departure from theology he inherited from medieval Catholicism. Along the way to these components, Luther's theology underwent a gradual evolution away from his earliest influences to arrive at his own unique characteristic contributions. He also acknowledged the superiority of his later writings and rejected some of his own earlier work. Later writings, after approximately 1525, typically involved increased clarity, focus, and consistency rather than a complete change of heart. He was also influenced at different points by certain of his important predecessors. A few of these are discussed in this chapter.

Luther's theology emerged from late medieval scholasticism and was formed in reaction to the Church's penitential system. It was also influenced by a number of interlocutors along the way, primarily Augustine, the founder of his monastic order and theologian of great standing in the Catholic tradition. To that we can add the then-contemporary influence of a new school of philosophy that appeared on the scene to challenge the dominant Thomism of his era, namely nominalism.

Influences, Interlocuters, and Developments

Simply and briefly stated, nominalism is the view that universals and abstract objects don't really exist, except by name only, or only in the human mind. This was in opposition to both Platonism, which asserted that universals existed in a greater reality above particulars, and Aristotelianism, which asserted that universals subsisted within particular things. Luther adopted parts of the philosophical framework of nominalism as spearheaded by its founding light, William of Ockham, specifically some of its logic and epistemology. In particular, Ockham advanced the religious notion that something was good simply by virtue of it being declared (named) good by God, on account of value to it ascribed by God, rather than because of its intrinsic quality. So, justification could not be caused by human disposition on account of its own nature, as with Pelagius.[1] This was key for Luther's interpretation of Paul in the New Testament. Paul used the Greek word for "declare righteous" twelve times in his writings, but only once did he use the word for "make righteous" to expound his doctrine of justification. Luther eventually came to understand this philosophically via his background in nominalism. When Luther began his studies, Thomism (of Thomas Aquinas) had been the standard orthodox theology of the Roman Catholic Church since the twelfth century. Nominalism's challenge to it one hundred years later had been suppressed. However, in fifteenth century Germany it had been revived by Gabriel Biel, sometimes identified as the "last scholastic." Nominalism had become dominant at the University of Erfurt (in contrast to Thomism) by the time Luther arrived there as a student.[2]

Nominalism's primary religious proponent, Gabriel Biel, also later acted as a provocation to opposition by Luther and his followers because of Biel's synergism. Then, Erasmus of Rotterdam provided both Melanchthon and Luther with vocabulary and tools for extracting a reformational understanding of justification from their biblical studies. But he also provoked Luther, through argument and opposition, to arrive at final theological positions.

1. Chung, "Martin Luther and the Scholastics," 88.
2. Dragseth, *The Devil's Whore*, 3–6.

Finally, there is the later influence of Luther's partner in reform, Philip Melanchthon (addressed in the next chapter). Luther reached his stable theological positions after his exchanges with Melanchthon, and that influence had a significant bearing on the work of the later Lutheran theologians that composed the FC (that united the Lutheran churches in Germany years after Luther had passed from the scene). There are other influences and provocations that could be cited, including a variety of ancient theologians, Thomas Aquinas, the mystic Johannes Tauler, Scottish philosopher Duns Scotus, several biblical humanists, Johann Eck, and even Luther's own superior and confessor in the Augustinian order, Johann von Staupitz. In the following paragraphs I limit my description to a few selected important interlocutors that left a mark on or stimulated the development of what Luther's theology would finally become.

PETER LOMBARD, GABRIEL BIEL, AND ANSELM

Gabriel Biel has the distinction of being one of the very few individual theologians specifically named and criticized in the *Lutheran Confessions*. This occurs three times in Melanchthon's *Apology of the Augsburg Confession*. In addition, Biel is quite often alluded to indirectly, assumed to be a prime representative of the late medieval scholastic theology harshly criticized therein. Luther also criticizes him by name thirteen times in his 1517 *Disputation Against Scholastic Theology*.[3]

It is constructive to compare the marginal notes to Peter Lombard's *Sentences* recorded by Gabriel Biel, with those made by Martin Luther to his own copy of that same standard medieval theological textbook. At this early stage in Luther's career (these notes in fact being his earliest surviving written work), the disagreements with either Lombard or Biel are not so sharply drawn. We can however clearly see their disagreement over the concept of original sin, which surely had an influence on the later development

3. LW 31:1–16.

of Luther's understanding of justification. Not only that, it can be seen how Luther clearly disagreed with the general Augustinian and ancient majority consensus of theologians about the nature and transmission of original sin. I will attempt to describe the essential point of this disagreement, while avoiding the intricate and arcane reasoning around the archaic understanding of human physiology (such as humors, heat, tinder, and seeds) used in constructing arguments at the time. As a result, some nuance will undoubtedly be missing. Another striking feature of Luther's notes is his strong hostility to philosophers (particularly Aristotle), by implication from the context, even though it is questionable just how conversant in detail he really was with the medieval scholastics and earlier philosophers at this point in time. The following discussion in the remainder of this subsection is derived from an essay containing a detailed analysis by Lawrence F. Murphy, S.J.[4]

Peter Lombard in his *Sentences*, considered whether sin entered the world through an actual sin in imitation of Adam's disobedience (as Abelard might have it) or something transmitted by propagation from common origins. He sides with Augustine—the propagation was through inheriting the flesh defiled by concupiscence when exercised. He goes on to argue that original sin involves not merely a debt of punishment for Adam's disobedience, but actual inherited guilt as well, even though it is not from an actual personal sin. He believed, like Augustine, that all men were materially present in Adam. Then, following transmission of a small part of Adam's substance to his offspring and descendants, it propagates in humanity by "multiplication of nature," without the addition of any external substance, such as food. For proof of this, reference was made to the multiplication of the loaves and fishes miracle recorded in the gospels, and the account of Eve being made from Adam's rib in Genesis. Luther highlights the loaves miracle in his marginal notes and approves Lombard's explanation in contradiction to Biel and others on this point.

Since the time when Lombard's *Sentences* was written (1150), theologians had gravitated more toward Anselm's view that original

---

4. Murphy, "Martin Luther and Gabriel Biel," 52–72.

sin is the lack or loss of original justice rather than a thing in itself, like a stain on the soul. Gabriel Biel, in his *Commentary on the Sentences*, follows Ockham in explaining original justice as a supernatural gift that causes perfect tranquility in the soul related to its powers (of the will). But without this original justice, rebellion against the perfect will and right reason is natural. Concupiscence, then, inclines the soul to take delight in the flesh, repressing spiritual delights. This is very much congruent with Augustine's description of misdirected love. Biel tries to reconcile Augustine with Anselm by saying that original sin as concupiscence is the material element, whereas the lack of original justice is the formal element.

Interestingly, Luther's marginal notes shows that he agrees with Anselm, and is therefore in (rare) disagreement with Augustine, in this case on the nature of original sin. He rejects also any ideas from Lombard, Biel, and Ockham that a positively existing quality (such as a "stain") is needed to explain original sin. He sees sin as only a negative deprivation. He even uses a radical syllogism to state that because evil is nothing, and sin is evil, therefore sin is nothing. He is here referring to sinfulness in corrupted human nature, not the sinful acts manifested from it. So, he is repeating the claim that sin in that sense is nothing in itself, but is only a deprivation (of original justice), as Anslem before him claimed. He also notes that according to Lombard, Adam's guilt has the consequence of debt (for that guilt) upon all his descendants. "That is why the flesh is concupiscent, because it is deserted by grace and virtue."[5] An important implication inveighing against philosophy in theology is also seen by the occurrence of the phrase "the masks of the philosophers" in Luther's notes. He almost certainly had Aristotle especially in mind, whose reasoning he believed obscured, distorted, or was downright contrary to the gospel.

Luther and the reformers' condemnation of Gabriel Biel was occasioned by what they thought were statements that marked him unequivocally as a Pelagian. Biel distinguished between God's absolute and ordered power. The ordered power includes the promise

---

5. Murphy, "Martin Luther and Gabriel Biel," (translated quotation from Luther's notation to Lombard's *Sentences*).

that God will save those who do their very best. The granting of grace was the result of good works rather than vice-versa. According to Biel, the "absolute love of God is within reach of natural man without the assistance of grace."[6] He makes no distinction between human will before or after The Fall, though it makes it harder to obey God. But not impossible. Biel taught justification by divine acceptance—justification by naturally possible good works that God graciously promises to accept, rather than by grace or faith.[7] For Luther, this stance of Biel negated the whole purpose of Christ's Incarnation and death. Acceptance, however, was associated with the inhabitation of the Holy Spirit in each believer.[8] So, no distinction was made by Biel or other scholastics of this period between justification and sanctification.

ERASMUS OF ROTTERDAM

Erasmus provided two kinds of influence for Luther and Melanchthon in the development of Reformation theology. First was his biblical scholarship, providing tools the reformers used in theirs. Erasmus' critical edition of the New Testament (1516) in the original Greek was the best source available and was an important advance over the Latin Vulgate, a translation that had long been in standard use by the church in the West. The new linguistic tools for study enabled the reformers to recover original meanings of key terminology.

Luther acknowledged in his *Explanations for the Ninety-Five Theses* (1518) that he had gotten his concept of repentance via Erasmus' correction of the Vulgate (repent rather than "do penance")[9]. Two other terms of utmost importance for Luther were grace and faith. In Catholic theology of the time, grace was conceived of as a divine substance that could be poured and infused into the soul, as

---

6. Oberman, *Harvest of Medieval Theology*, 133.
7. Oberman, *Harvest of Medieval Theology*, 183.
8. Oberman, *Harvest of Medieval Theology*, 353–56.
9. LW 48:66.

a sort of healing medicine for the sickness of sin. The more grace a person had, the more righteous they became internally and intrinsically. Erasmus recovered the meaning of grace as the favorable attitude of God toward a person, a type of divine kindness. Luther associated this divine favor closely with a determination on the part of God to forgive. Refer to my discussion of the Christus Victor motif for atonement in chapter 3, in the section titled *Forgiveness of Sin and Eternal Life*. Swedish theologian Gustave Aulén advocated the idea that this viewpoint was found in Luther, as a revival of this classic, "dramatic" motif over Anselm's satisfaction theory.

Erasmus also properly distinguished the (Latin) words imputare (extrinsic qualities) and reputare (intrinsic qualities) as early as 1503, about which there had been some confusion. He wrote in his *Enchiridion* that "Christ will fight for you and impute (reckon) his gift to you as merit." And in his 1522 paraphrase of Rom 3:22, he commented: "For to be imputed, or rendered acceptable, is, properly speaking, not that the debt has been paid off in fact, but that notwithstanding one has been released, out of imputed benignity."[10] He didn't elaborate the idea further, or make a direct connection with a forensic interpretation of justification as such. But Luther picked up on this language eventually and gained clarity, when (with Melanchthon's help) he made the distinction between two kinds of righteousness: extrinsic (by imputation of Christ's merit) and intrinsic (by the progressive transformative influence of the Holy Spirit).[11]

Regarding the definition of faith, Erasmus treated it as a synonym for trust as early as 1518, albeit a trust grounded in future hope of ultimate salvation, similar to Gabriel Biel's conception of hope. This understanding was repeated in his 1522 paraphrase of Rom 3:22 and in his later *Annotations*.[12] This was something of a new interpretation because the medieval view held that this kind of trust could have a negative connotation of false security. Luther would have shared that view, at least up until the point (in late

10. Green, "Influence of Erasmus," 187.
11. Green, "Influence of Erasmus," 185.
12. Green, *How Melanchthon Helped Luther*, 143–44.

1518) that he first connected God's promise of salvation in Christ with certainty. Still, he warned against a false kind of confidence in outward works.[13] Luther often spoke of justification in other ways, with different metaphors and associations, such as spiritual marriage with Christ (the happy exchange), creation from nothing, and (echoing Anselm's penal substitutionary theory of the Atonement) making recompense for the insult to God's honor by sin. In fact, Luther took issue with Erasmus over imputation (in 1522), which he said was unacceptable if considered apart from Christ's work of atonement.

The other major contribution of Erasmus was his provocation of Luther regarding the issue of free will. For a while, Erasmus had been somewhat supportive of Luther in the sense that they both advocated reforms in the Church, and wanted to address the corruption. In 1524, though, Erasmus published *On the Free Will: Discourses or Comparisons* and came out against Luther. This initiated back-and-forth mutual rebuttals in print, with Luther by the end of 1525 producing what some consider his masterwork, *On the Bondage of the Will*. Erasmus argued against predestination (while acknowledging God's foreknowledge and omniscience) by claiming that baptism, repentance, and conversion depended on an exercise of free will. Accordingly, without free will, the purpose of the law and divine justice are both negated; without these, there can't be any just eternal reward or punishment. In his view, the human will was weakened by The Fall, but still survived in an operative fashion. Erasmus argued that the biblical discourse on this was not decisive and could be interpreted differently in different passages to argue on opposite sides of the question.[14] He further explained his view by saying that grace first called, led, and assisted people to know, then to choose, enabling action leading to salvation. Erasmus' definition of free choice was this (as quoted by Luther): "By free choice in this place we mean a power of the human will by which one can apply oneself to the things which

---

13. LW 27:223.
14. Leppin, "Introduction to *The Bondage of the Will*," 154.

lead to eternal salvation, or turn away from them."[15] It should be noted that with this definition, Erasmus was not discounting the enabling power of God's grace, but intended to emphasize human responsibility.

In *On the Bondage of the Will*, Luther countered that nobody could achieve salvation through willpower, so deeply and hopelessly mired in sin and ignorance as they were. Instead, God unilaterally changes a person (monergism). "The righteousness of faith . . . does not consist in any works, but in the favorableness of God, and in God's imputation through grace." Luther argued vehemently against Erasmus, asserting that Erasmus' "middle way," wherein a little bit of power or effectiveness for achieving righteousness is ascribed to (a weakened) free will so as to resolve contradictions in scripture, led nowhere. Crediting God alone for everything was the only way to harmonize scripture and eliminate contradiction.[16] Luther pointedly differed from Erasmus over the function of the law (the Ten Commandments). Erasmus believed that a command assumed the ability to perform the duty—God would not command someone to do something that they were not able to do. Luther contended that the commandments were given to show exactly the opposite—driving one to despair of one's own efforts, acknowledge helplessness, and to seek mercy in God's grace (the second use of the law).

Additional issues were settled for Luther in the writing of this treatise, such as the primacy and centrality of scripture for authority in the Church, and a distinction between the hidden and revealed God. The revealed God was the one known in Jesus Christ and in the scriptures. Other notions about God apart from this were speculative and to be avoided.

Finally, Erasmus also acted as a catalyst for Melanchthon's development of the doctrine of justification and thereby influenced Luther indirectly in that manner. Melanchthon's influence is considered in more detail in the next two chapters.

---

15. LW 33:102–3.
16. LW 33: 245–46.

Influences, Interlocuters, and Developments

AUGUSTINE OF HIPPO

At many points, the influence of Augustine can be seen in Luther's lecturing, writing, and theological development—particularly in early work before 1519. Luther moved away from the scholasticism of his day via the discovery of the older theology expounded by Augustine. Though the law/gospel distinction is rooted in Paul's writings, the distinction Luther eventually made between law and gospel was initiated by his reading of Augustine's distinction between law and grace in the treatise *On the Spirit and the Letter*, published in 412. A kind of equivalency can be seen where Augustine explained that the letter kills but the spirit gives life. Luther liked to say that a person is killed by the law's demands, though the law is good in itself as being God's requirement regarding human behavior. People hear and absorb the letter of the law and naturally try to fulfill it in an effort at self-justification. But they cannot, and it leads a person to psychological despair about their relationship to God.[17] This was Luther's intense experience of anfechtung, and matched the experiences he heard from fellow monks in their confessions. Augustine based his explanation on 2 Cor 3:4–6. He wrote: "Through the law a man is shown his weakness, that through faith he may flee to God's mercy and be healed."[18] Augustine made a parallel distinction between what he called the law of works and the law of faith: "We conclude that a man is not justified by the precepts of a good life, except through faith in Jesus Christ; that is, not by the law of works, but by the law of faith; not of the Letter, but of the Spirit; not through the merits of things done, but by grace, freely."[19] In Luther's commentary on Romans (1515–16), he quotes from *On the Spirit and the Letter* twenty-seven times and frequently from other works of Augustine,[20] thus illustrating the heavy influence by his order's founder at that stage of his

---

17. Dragseth, "Spirit and Letter, Gospel and Law," 30–32.

18. Augustine, *On the Spirit and the Letter*, 51.

19. Green, *How Melanchthon Helped Luther*, 86 (Luther quotation trans. from Latin).

20. Green, *How Melanchthon Helped Luther*, 87.

Ontological and Imputed Righteousness

thinking. He takes up Augustine's idea contrasting works of the law with works of faith specifically in his early lectures on *Romans* and *Galatians* (1515–17). In his commentary on Rom 3:20, Luther contends that works of law are performed under compulsion or a desire to gain salvation, but that works of faith are done freely out of love, a spirit of freedom, and a genuine heartfelt desire to be pleasing toward God.[21]

Augustine spent much of his lifetime in theological work effectively battling his main opponents—the Manicheans, the Donatists, and most significantly for Luther—Pelagius. Pelagius was condemned by the Catholic Church for heresy by 415, but Luther, after reading Augustine's writings against Pelagius, came to realize that the medieval theologians were for the most part exhibiting a continuing influence of Pelagianism.[22]

Augustine attempted to reconcile the paradoxical notions of predestination and free will by elaborating (following the earlier Tertullian) the concept of original sin in his interpretation of the story of The Fall in *Genesis*. While he referenced and performed exegeses on passages from scripture (particularly Rom 5:12–21) to try to prove his position, his strongest and most repeated argument was an appeal to the Church's universal practice of infant baptism. He consistently argued that its practice was from necessity because of original sin.[23] According to his concept, all of humanity is imputed and tainted with the guilt of Adam's sin, with concupiscence being transmitted through biological reproduction down through all subsequent generations. With this biological transmission thesis, he was going beyond what the Apostle Paul said in scripture by trying to explain exactly how sin was transmitted to Adam's descendants. He believed that humans in their fallen condition are unable to do or even will to do the good by their own efforts.[24] This was the basis of his opposition to the Pelagians, who believed that although Adam sinned, sin could be regarded as a

21. Luther, "Lectures on Romans 3:20–27," 485.
22. LW 30: Ch. 2, para. 11.50.
23. McGonigle, "Augustine v Pelagius on Original Sin," 48.
24. Tornau, "Augustine of Hippo," para. 7.6.

bad example, which a person could ignore if they chose. A person could turn to God with their inherent (created by God) free will, doing what is within them.[25] Biel interpreted this axiom from Pelagius to mean that on that basis God was required to remit sin and grant the initial grace by virtue of a covenant with humanity to do so.[26] Pelagius denied both original sin and predestination, arguing for responsibility of human beings to obey God's commands instead of making excuses. Augustine argued for something he called "prevenient grace," a concept that has endured in Catholic theology. One can readily see how Luther found encouragement from Augustine in his battles with scholastic theologians such as Gabriel Biel, and even later with Erasmus (regarding free will) and others. The idea of prevenient grace seems quite close to Luther's explanation of the third article of the creed in his Small Catechism: "I believe that by my own understanding or strength I cannot believe in Jesus Christ my Lord or come to him, but instead the Holy Spirit has called me through the gospel, enlightened me with his gifts . . . "[27] Augustine distinguished between the faculty and the use of free will, parallel to distinguishing the capacity and inclination to sin stemming from concupiscence, from actual sin committed in acts. Somewhat in line with Luther's explanation, he thought that a person could exercise the will to believe in Christ, but only when given the power to believe from outside and above.

Augustine thought that after The Fall, the human person is free only to choose disobedience and other manifestations of sin[28] (similarly to Luther's idea about the human will). He argued that people cannot turn to God on their own. They need an initial infusion of grace to be able to do that—with God's grace, free will lost in The Fall is at least partially restored and prepares one to accept further grace from God, in a progressive manner, by the faith so generated.

As regards predestination, which Augustine also propounded, the question then was, who is given the prevenient grace, and

25. MacCulloch, *Christianity*, 307.
26. Chung, "Martin Luther and the Scholastics," 89.
27. Kolb and Wengert, *Book of Concord,* 355.
28. McGonigle, "Augustine v Pelagius on Original Sin," 46.

who would be among the elect? That would appear to be God's mysterious and arbitrary choice, but not to be considered unjust, because all are guilty and deserve condemnation on account of Adam's sin. Adam stood as a representative of all humankind, as Jesus would when he came to be considered the perfectly sinless and righteous "second Adam." Augustine had the view that not only concupiscence was inherited, but also a legal sentence of condemnation passed on from Adam's condemnation.[29] Undoubtedly, along with Paul's juridical metaphor, this helped pave the way for a solution to that condemnation by the classic Protestant doctrine of forensic justification.

The doctrine of election was taken up by Luther and Calvin during the Reformation. Calvin taught a "double predestination" of both the elect and the damned, credited to God's absolute sovereignty and glory. Luther held that the elect are predestined to salvation, but he wouldn't attribute predestination of the lost. He believed, like Calvin, in God's sovereignty, but God's choices in that regard concerned his hidden will, something humans were not to be concerned with in a speculative manner. It was enough that God had revealed his loving desire (in the scriptures) that all be redeemed, and that people should cling to that with certainty for comfort and assurance.

Debates continued after Augustine had offered his solution, and it continued through Christian history to have a lasting influence, especially in the Catholic Church—that "we have lost our natural ability to self-determination, which can only be repaired and restored by the divine grace that has manifested itself in the Incarnation and sacrifice of Christ and works inwardly to free our will from its enslavement to sin."[30] This is congruent with the Tridentine Roman Catholic position that God's grace is "infused" into the soul for its salvation. This isn't the same as Luther's external grace of the external Word, an alien righteousness that comes from outside, but is a step in the direction of giving God all the credit, in contrast to earlier views that assumed salvation results from

---

29. McGonigle, "Augustine v Pelagius on Original Sin," 47.
30. Tornau, "Augustine of Hippo," para. 7.6.

the cooperation of divine grace and human initiative, said to be standard in early Christianity since Origen.[31] The medieval understanding of justification was that persons were made righteous in the sight of God through a fundamental change in their natures, not merely their status. Justification was seen as a process. Thomas Aquinas understood this as a process in terms of Aristotelian physics. The movement of the prime mover came first, followed by the movement of that which was to be moved, followed by termination of the movement when the objective of the movement had been reached. Accordingly, Thomas described a four-fold framework for justification. First is infusion of grace by God. Second is the movement of human free will toward God. Third is its recoil from sin and the fourth (last) is the remission of guilt.[32]

But Augustine, like Paul, then later Luther, excluded human merit or works (of the law) from consideration—everything depended on God's pure grace. In his *Treatise on the Spirit and the Letter*, although he was unclear about imputation (as Luther later noted in 1545), Augustine advanced the idea of the believer being clothed in Christ's righteousness.

In the next chapter, I consider Luther's greatest influencer of all, with reference to the doctrine of justification. Luther made his initial reformational breakthrough around the time of Melanchthon's arrival to teach on the Wittenburg faculty in 1518. Melanchthon soon began to take up Luther's cause of reform and subsequently published some very significant works that systematized his colleague's theology in more formal fashion. But it turned out to be a two-way exchange between them. Luther came to greater clarity and focus on the passive, external imputed righteousness through that exchange. This trajectory of development laid the groundwork for the eventual classical doctrine articulated in the *Lutheran Confessions*. To that end, I reference Melanchthon's most important works, namely *Loci Communes*, *The Augsburg Confession*, and *The Apology of the Augsburg Confession*.

---

31. Tornau, "Augustine of Hippo," para. 7.6.
32. Chung, "Martin Luther and the Scholastics," 86–87.

5

Melanchthon and Luther

MELANCHTHON HAS BEEN A somewhat controversial figure in Lutheran history, which is rather ironic since he courted controversy far less, at least by intention, than Luther did during his life and career. He was much more irenic in his approach and sometimes sought compromise in the interest of preserving the unity of the Church, whether in dialog with representatives of the Church of Rome or with Reformed theologians and leaders. After Luther died, factions developed within the Lutheran churches. One group coalesced around those who followed Melanchthon as their leading light (the Philipists) and another group who opposed them, claiming to represent Luther more authentically (the Gnesio-Lutherans).

Luther thought so highly of Melanchthon's *Loci Communes Theologici* (December 1521) that he once said it should be incorporated into the canon of Christian scripture. This seems like a bit of hyperbole, but Luther also once said that Melanchthon was the greatest theologian that had ever lived. Attitudes in the Lutheran churches since then have been decidedly mixed. However, he was an important scholar and certainly made very key contributions historically. Now we will consider Melanchthon's influence on Luther prior to his composition of the AC and its *Apology*.

Melanchthon articulated his forensic view of the doctrine of justification by 1519, derived from his interpretation of Paul's epistle to the *Romans*. This interpretation went on in Lutheran history to become part of its confessional and systematic theological structure. Also, according to Melanchthon this interpretation was incomplete without the additional explanation that this kind of justification resulted in a changed will to be able to give love, respond to grace with good works, and share the message of God's grace to others in the gospel message.[1] Melanchthon also contributed to the development of Luther's transformed vocabulary post-1518 (the year Melanchthon came to teach at Wittenberg University) for words such as grace, faith, justification, sanctification, law, and gospel. In reformational rhetoric these words were defined differently than in both Augustinian and medieval scholastic usage. Much of that difference can be attributed to Melanchthon's recovery of original Biblical language and his humanist scholarship. Prime examples are: the definition of grace as God's favorable attitude toward a person or persons, as opposed to a regenerating substance poured into a repentant individual's soul. Faith was defined as ultimate trust in God rather than an intellectual acceptance of the Church's official teachings (à la Gabiel Biel) and prescriptions for pious behavior. The language of imputation used to explicate the doctrine of justification was developed by Melanchthon and highly influenced Luther's understanding. Despite their independent and at times differing perspectives, this ultimately united them and their subsequent followers in the Lutheran and Protestant movements for a considerable time.

Through his biblical studies, Melanchthon transformed the classical humanist focus on man as the measure of all things into the reformational understanding of God as the measure of all things. In the estimation of Werner Elert, the late Professor of Church History and Systematic Theology at the University of Erlangen, "In the language of the doctrine of justification . . . [that measure] did not exist on the basis of how he judged himself, but of how God judged him instead . . . Only in the purely forensic

---

1. Keith, Preface to *How Melanchthon Helped Luther*, xvii-xix.

understanding of our justification before God, as we owe it to Melanchthon, is the full hardness of the situation preserved, that we have to answer for everything before God."[2]

Melanchthon arrived in Wittenberg in August 1518, newly hired as professor of Greek at the University. He wound up teaching philology and theology as well. He had almost certainly heard of the *Ninety-Five Theses* of the previous year (and the indulgence controversy that followed) before actually meeting Luther for the first time when he arrived. He kept up a correspondence with Erasmus, who had great admiration for the young scholar, and who had already commented on the *Ninety-Five Theses*, which of course had circulated all over Europe within a month of its initial transmission to Archbishop Albert of Mainz.

In his inaugural address in the All Saints' (Castle) Church in Wittenberg on August 28, 1518, he decried the scholastic pupils of Aquinas that he believed had misinterpreted and corrupted Aristotle, arguing for a return to the sources and a restoration of what he called the "true Aristotle."[3] He became Germany's leading humanist during his career, as well as the leading systematician of Lutheran theology. Luther once called Aristotle "that damned pagan," but despite his ultimate disdain for Aristotle and the philosophers, he didn't have any objection to Melanchthon's methods as a biblical humanist scholar, and greatly admired his work. As Melanchthon became more closely aligned with Luther, his opinion of Aristotle (and philosophy in general) changed, taking a very negative turn. He instead began to champion the Apostle Paul, the patron of the theological faculty at Wittenberg, as superior to all the philosophers.

---

2. Elert, "Humanitat und Kirche," 101, 103 [Trans. by Lowell C. Green in *How Melanchthon Helped Luther*, 109].

3. Green, *How Melanchthon Helped Luther*, 120 [Melanchthon quote trans. from German].

EARLY WORK AND DOCTRINE

In September 1519, Melanchthon obtained the degree that gave him the right to teach biblical courses in theology at the university. For this he had prepared his *Baccalaureate Theses*, which consisted of exegetical work and some early systematic theology that had evolved from his studies of *Romans*. Notably, it features the first reformational assertion of justification by the free imputation of Christ's merit to the believer.[4]

Melanchthon's earliest written work on justification is found in his *Theological Institutes*, developed in 1518–19. In it, he understands sin in a manner closer to Augustine than to the medieval scholastics, identifying it with corruption of the heart (lust or concupiscence), self-love, and original sin. According to Melanchthon, a person's natural reaction upon realization of sinfulness is to try to overcome it by better outward performance of the requirements of the law. This is suggested by natural reason, but is futile because the law can't help, only driving an individual further into sin. Here he echoes Luther's view of the law. He also follows Paul in asserting that the letter kills and the law leads to wrath. Melanchthon argues that this is because neither the powers of reason nor the human can effect a change of the heart. For justification there must be a surrender of the human will to God.[5] In this early work, Melanchthon, like Augustine (and Luther at this point) still identified grace as a substance and a work of inner renewal and purification by the Holy Spirit. He speaks of faith in a different way than the medieval scholastics with their distinction of the theological virtues of faith, hope, and love. Melanchthon writes, "Faith is the firm belief in the divine word; by faith we are enlightened and God is shown to us."[6] He gave Luther this insight and motivation in 1518 shortly after they met. This put them on the path to future developments in the Reformation theology of justification.

---

4. Green, *How Melanchthon Helped Luther*, 125–26.

5. Melanchthon, *Corpus Reformatorum (CR) 1834*, 21:52 [Trans. by Lowell C. Green in *How Melanchthon Helped Luther,* 130].

6. Melanchthon, *CR 1834*, 21:53 [Trans. Green, 132].

Oswald Bayer located the appearance of promisio in Luther's writing as early as the summer of 1518, in his fifty theses of the disputation *For the Investigation of Truth and for the Comfort of Troubled Consciences*. By October, this was highlighted as the reformational breakthrough discovery when it became the main point of contention between Luther and official representatives of the Roman church. As mentioned in chapter 2, Luther met to discuss his *Ninety-Five Theses* with Cardinal Cajetan at Augsburg on October 7, 1518. In the course of the three-day period of discussion, Luther reached the definitive point of regarding saving faith as specific faith in the certainty of salvation for Christ's sake, in the present moment rather than only a hope for the future. This is documented in his report of that time, the *Acta Augustana*. Luther explicitly stated that his new understanding of faith and justification had been aided by Melanchthon, and their exchanges on the topic of faith had apparently happened in the short time between Melanchthon's arrival at Wittenburg (August) and Luther's trip to Augsburg (October).[7] In his early lectures on *Romans* and *Hebrews*, he used (among others) the traditional Latin term *credulitas* (acceptance) to indicate a kind of subjective faithfulness, in contrast to objective faith.[8] This includes the concept of the indwelling of God with activity in a person's heart.[9]

The corresponding new understanding of grace was more gradual in both its development and in its documented appearance in Luther's theology. Until late in 1518, Luther, like his Catholic predecessors, viewed grace as a gift imparted to the believer internally as a sanctifying, healing medicine for the disease of sin, leading to justification. This view eventually (and completely) gave way to the idea of grace as God's kind attitude of unmerited favor and mercy for the sake of Christ. But it took several years to thoroughly work out. Melanchthon seems to have gotten there first, likely under the linguistic influence of Erasmus, and in his intense interest in developing correct definitions and proper methods. He

---

7. Green, *How Melanchthon Helped Luther*, 149.
8. Green, *How Melanchthon Helped Luther*, 140.
9. Green, *How Melanchthon Helped Luther*, 142.

no doubt influenced Luther to proceed in this direction in understanding grace. As late as 1519, in his first, shorter *Galatians* commentary (see verse 3:7), Luther had rejected grace as simply divine favor.[10] Two years later in his treatise against Latomus, he had come to a new view, and in it he impressed Melanchthon with the idea that Christians were simultaneously sinners and justified. Then, in 1523 when Luther published a revision of his *Galatians* commentary, he removed the earlier criticism of grace as divine favor.

In his *Annotations on Romans* (1520), Melanchthon defined the gospel as proclamation of grace, and grace as the mercy of God . . . and reception of benefits through Christ, the favor of God. Melanchthon's description of grace as God's favor appeared in February 1521 when he published a treatise defending Luther against Thomas Rhadino.[11] Definitively, and advancing further, in his *Loci Communes* Melanchthon developed his theological system (the first Protestant dogmatics) around this conception of grace, distinguishing grace from the gifts of grace. He stated, "The word for grace does not signify any condition in us, but rather the same gracious will or benevolence of God toward us . . . In conclusion, grace is nothing other than forgiveness or remission of sin. The gift is the Holy Spirit, regenerating and sanctifying the heart."[12]

THE *LOCI COMMUNES*

It is well known how enthusiastic Luther was about this work and without a doubt it commanded an important influence on his thinking. He had declared it as one of the clearest statements of the Christian religion ever written. "There's no book under the sun in which the whole of theology is so compactly presented as in the *Loci Communes*. If you read all the fathers and sententiaries you have nothing. No better book has been written after the Holy

---

10. LW 27:252.
11. Green, *How Melanchthon Helped Luther*, 159.
12. Melanchthon, *Loci Communes Theologici*, 88.

Scriptures than Philip's. He expresses himself more concisely than I do."[13] If this is thought now to be hyperbolic, it does stand as Melanchthon's most important work aside from the AC. Additionally, inspired by Luther, it strove to demonstrate the corruption of the reigning theology of the scholastics, "who have offered us the subtleties of Aristotle instead of the teachings of Christ."[14]

The *Loci* wouldn't be considered systematic theology in the modern sense. Its stated purpose was to provide an outline and compendium of essential concepts and topics, collected together in "nests" for students to pursue in their studies. Erasmus had often recommended this as a theological method[15] —the difference being that Melanchthon wished this effort to proceed from the scriptural texts alone as the source and standard. It expressed Pauline thought derived mainly from *Romans* and *Galatians*, and was predominantly concerned with themes of sin, grace, law, and gospel.[16] The *Loci Communes* later wound up functioning as a summary of the teachings of the Lutheran Reformation.

Here are a few references to what it had to say about Justification and Faith, one of the main topics in the *Loci Communes*. It is important to keep in mind that Melanchthon later changed some of his ideas and took occasion to revise and eventually greatly expand the text. Two more major editions were published in his lifetime. The points that follow are taken from the first edition, published in December 1521, since that is within the time period under consideration in this chapter.

Faith is personal trust in God's promise of mercy and forgiveness rather than any historical knowledge. It is "an affectation of the heart."[17] Justification happens when a person understands and believes he or she is forgiven.[18] Melanchthon also emphasizes regeneration by the Holy Spirit. The Christian is in the process

---

13. LW 54:440.
14. Melanchthon, *Loci*, 19.
15. Erasmus, *On Copia of Words and Ideas*, 291.
16. Pauck, "Editor's Introduction" to Melanchthon, *Loci*, 12, 14.
17. Melanchthon, *Loci*, 90.
18. Melanchthon, *Loci*, 105.

of being sanctified. "Christianity is freedom . . . Those who have been renewed by the spirit of Christ now conform voluntarily even without the law to what the law used to command."[19]

"Therefore, we are justified when, put to death by the law, we are made alive again by the word of grace promised in Christ; the gospel forgives our sins, and we cling to Christ in faith, not doubting in the least that the righteousness of Christ is our righteousness . . . But faith alone in the mercy and grace of God in Jesus Christ is our righteousness."[20]

Melanchthon begins his biblical exposition and defense of the doctrine by referencing Rom 4:5 and Gen 15:6 regarding Abraham being reckoned righteous because of his faith (trust).[21] He goes on to explain that a person that believes and trusts in God's mercy fulfills the law gladly and willingly, performing good works unmotivated by fear, trusting without looking or paying any attention to them.[22] He cites more scriptural examples and proofs of what he is saying, as well as mentioning Luther's treatise *On the Freedom of a Christian* as an example in further praise of the power of the faith-as-trust concept. He mainly distinguishes the Old Testament promises as material in nature, and those in the New Testament as spiritual. Nevertheless, both types provide occasion for the response and illustration of faith.[23] Melanchthon running through scripture passages in this way brings to mind Luther's description of doing something similar after his reformational discovery, recounted in 1545 as his tower experience. There he reports finding confirmation of his new realizations and insight into Paul at every turn as he went back over key scriptural passages. It is clear that whatever differences there were between the two men, their minds at this point were running on the same track, with mutual influence. Melanchthon executes his scriptural survey in the *Loci Communes* with great clarity, specificity, and thoroughness. It was this

19. Melanchthon, *Loci*, 123.
20. Melanchthon, *Loci*, 88–89.
21. Melanchthon, *Loci*.
22. Melanchthon, *Loci*, 93.
23. Melanchthon, *Loci*, 96.

comprehensive clarity that Luther and the Lutheran movement found so valuable.

As a rationale for the Lutheran theological perspective, Melanchthon gives a simple powerful syllogism: "Why is it that justification is attributed to faith alone? I answer that since we are justified by the mercy of God alone, and faith is clearly the recognition of that mercy by whatever promise you apprehend it, justification is attributed to faith alone."[24]

This chapter has covered the early career of Melanchthon as well as his influence on Luther and vice-versa. The evolution of Luther's early theology has been referenced. In the next chapter, the doctrine of justification as expounded in the BC is examined. This includes Melanchthon's contributions in the AC and its *Apology*. It also looks at the FC and how it resolved intra-Lutheran conflict after he and Luther had passed from the scene. I attempt to show a congruence between the mature theologies of Luther and Melanchthon, with that of the Formula, regarding justification.

---

24. Melanchthon, *Loci*, 105.

6

The Lutheran Confessions

IN THIS ANALYSIS, I have divided Luther's theological career into three periods:

1. The Catholic Luther (1509–1518)
2. Transition to Reformational Viewpoints (1518–1525)
3. The Mature Luther (1525–1545)

CATECHISMS

During his mature period, Luther's theology had become stable, with original insights and innovations firmly established in lectures and writings. Although he remained a working professor at the University, he turned more of his attention to establishing, nurturing, and educating emergent Lutheran congregations and families, thereby helping to consolidate the movement. He began to write and subsequently publish (1529) the *Small Catechism* and *Large Catechism* for the purpose of aiding basic Christian instruction. The *Small Catechism* was promoted for the laity, while the *Large Catechism* was meant to benefit simple clergy, who at that time were often poorly trained. Both arose from catechetical preaching, and were developed in response to conditions observed during official visitations to parishes in electoral Saxony. The *Small Catechism* has endured over the ensuing centuries as the most popular Lutheran document, used universally in Lutheran churches to this day. Both catechisms were adopted into the BC in 1580, as parts of the official collection of confessional documents that united the Lutheran churches in Germany.

THE *AUGSBURG CONFESSION*

The next year (1530), Emperor Charles V asked his mostly independent territorial Lutheran princes to explain their religious commitments to an imperial diet to be held in the city of Augsburg late that spring. Their theologians, led by Luther and Melanchthon, prepared documents on issues pertaining to reforms being implemented in the territorial churches. Luther couldn't travel because he was under an imperial ban, so Melanchthon was tasked to lead the delegation. They had to deal with the *Four Hundred Four Articles for the Imperial Diet* at Augsburg, edited and prepared by prominent and learned Roman Catholic theologian Johann Eck. It was fiercely oppositional to the reformers, and lumped together citations from the Wittenburgers' writings, especially Luther's, with citations from other groups and individuals (such as Melanchthon, Zwingli, Bugenhagen, Bucer, Oecolampadius, Rhegius, and Karlstadt) criticizing the contemporary Roman Catholic Church. All of these critics were considered heretical by the Catholic side. As a result, Luther chose Melanchthon not only to address reforms, but also to demonstrate the catholicity and orthodoxy of the Lutheran churches and their commitment to tradition and scripture, while agreeing with the Roman Catholic Church where possible in condemning those particular teachings that both parties considered false. Melanchthon composed the articles contained in the AC for this purpose, utilizing and expanding upon materials previously prepared in documents such as *The Schwabach Articles*, *The Marburg Articles*, *The Torgau Articles*, Luther's *Confession Concerning Christ's Supper*, and *Instructions to the Visitors of the Clergy in the*

Electorate of Saxony.[1] On June 25, German and Latin versions of the AC that had been subscribed by seven Lutheran princes and two municipal governments were presented to the emperor and assembly at Augsburg. The text with an added preface was published in May 1531, and that edition has been used by Lutheran churches as foundational ever since.

Regarding the doctrine of justification, there is only one short two-sentence article (IV. *Concerning Justification*) that directly addresses this topic. "Furthermore, it is taught that we cannot obtain forgiveness of sin and righteousness before God through our merit, work, or satisfactions, but that we receive . . . out of grace for Christ's sake through faith when we believe that Christ has suffered for us . . . and that righteousness and eternal life are given to us. For God will regard and reckon this faith as righteousness in his sight." Secondly, Article VI (*Concerning the New Obedience*) states in its first sentence: "It is also taught that such faith should yield good fruit and good works and that a person must do such good works as God has commanded for God's sake but not place trust in them as if thereby to earn grace before God."[2]

Thirdly, a lengthy Article XX follows, *Concerning Faith and Good Works*, defending the Lutheran churches against deliberate misrepresentations and false accusations of prohibiting good works, by generally mentioning past Lutheran writings. These would have included publications such as Luther's *Treatise on Good Works* and the catechisms. Melanchthon in this article repeats and elaborates in greater detail what he stated succinctly in articles IV and VI as mentioned above, and gives examples of proper good works done in a spirit of obedience to God. These are contrasted with what he described as unnecessary works prescribed by the Church of the time. He also here emphasized peace and reconciliation with God obtained through faith and true, trusting belief—rather than mere assent to the truth.

---

1. Kolb and Wengert, "Editors' Introduction to the Augsburg Confession," in *The Book of Concord*, 28.
2. Melanchthon, "The Augsburg Confession," in *The Book of Concord*, 38, 40.

THE *CONFUTATION OF THE AUGSBURG CONFESSION*

Emperor Charles reacted by telling the Protestants to retract their errors and accept the doctrines expressed in the *Confutation of the Augsburg Confession*. This document was prepared by a group of twelve theologians that focused criticism article-by-article on the AC rather than continue the broader approach used in Eck's *Four Hundred Four Articles*.[3] This is a meticulous work, with arguments proceeding carefully on the basis of selected scriptures.

On Article IV (Justification), the *Confutation* condemns Pelagius, but rejects the idea that human merit has no role. "All Catholics admit that our works of themselves have no merit, but God's grace makes them worthy to earn eternal life." The Confutation accepts article VI on *The New Obedience* insofar as it affirms that faith bears fruit in good works. However, it denies that faith alone suffices for justification, contending that "the gospel does not exclude good works."[4] For Article XX on *Faith and Good Works*, the *Confutation* rejects the idea that good works do not merit the forgiveness of sins, and quotes scriptural passages that seem to indicate that good works and almsgiving effect a measure of atonement. Finally, it is claimed that the reformers' position also contradicts Augustine and "was rejected over a thousand years ago."[5]

THE *APOLOGY OF THE AUGSBURG CONFESSION*

A second (revised) German version of the *Confutation* was read to the imperial diet on August 3. Melanchthon and company (including the princes) had been denied a printed copy unless they agreed beforehand to submit to it, accept it, and not respond with a rebuttal. Needless to say, they refused. The *Confutation* wasn't

---

3. Graybill, *Honeycomb Scroll*, 324.

4. Kolb and Nestigen, "Confutation of the Augsburg Confession," in *Sources and Contexts*, 109.

5. Kolb and Nestigen, "Confutation," 118.

formally printed and published until 1559! Fortunately for them, the Lutheran party managed to transcribe the oral presentation. The transcription's substantial accuracy was verified twenty-nine years later when the *Confutation* was officially published and printed. In the more immediate time frame, the transcribed oral presentation of the *Confutation* provided the basis for Melanchthon to compose his *Apology of the Augsburg Confession*, with its first edition appearing in May 1531, fifteen months after the presentation of the AC. Melanchthon revised the *Apology* (and incorporated some suggestions from Luther) for a second edition (September) and that is the version adopted in 1580 for the BC.

In contrast to the brevity of the article (IV) on justification in the AC, the treatment of this article in the *Apology* goes on at length (perhaps 100 times longer) with its arguments. There is no rebuttal for article VI (as there was no direct disagreement) and a mercifully shorter treatment (five paragraphs) for article XX on *Good Works*. In the *Apology*, Melanchthon notably foregrounds sola fide, which would have been more characteristic of Luther's approach. He discusses the distinction between law and gospel, and proceeds to outline three component parts of the reformational doctrine of justification: "the promise itself; the fact that the promise is free; and the merits of Christ as the payment and atoning sacrifice."[6]

In certain places in the *Apology*, Melanchthon moves increasingly toward a forensic concept of justification, apprehended by faith, while seeming also to uphold the idea of God both declaring as well as making a sinner righteous through regeneration. "And because 'to be justified' means that out of unrighteous people righteous people are made or regenerated, it also means that they are pronounced or regarded as righteous. For scripture speaks both ways."[7] At the same time, he tries to make clear that justification is extrinsic, that good works don't play a part in it, while quoting Paul to prove his point. "God cannot be dealt with and grasped in any other way than through the Word . . . just as Paul notes: 'The

---

6. Melanchthon, "Apology of the Augsburg Confession," in *Sources and Contexts*, 128.

7. Melanchthon, "Apology," 132.

gospel is the power of God for salvation to everyone who has faith (Rom 1:16) . . . faith comes from what is heard (Rom 10:17).'" He then makes another syllogism: "Faith justifies because if justification takes place only through the Word and the Word is grasped only by faith, it follows that faith justifies . . . We have discussed these so far in order to show how regeneration takes place."[8] Later, he says: "To be sure, love and good works ought to follow faith . . . However, trust in the merit of love or works in justification is excluded."[9] He goes on to link justification with forgiveness of sin and God's reconciliation with people for Christ's sake because of his atoning sacrifice. He also makes plain that Paul's argument about justification apart from the law refers to the entire law (centering on the Ten Commandments, not on its ceremonial aspects) as Augustine also contended in his *On the Spirit and the Letter*; and furthermore, that Paul repeats these assertions consistently across his various epistles.[10] The seeming contradiction or ambiguity in the *Apology* between a declarative, forensic righteousness and one that came about from or with regeneration or renewal (sometimes referred to as effective justification) would be fully clarified and resolved for orthodox Lutheranism in the FC of 1577.

BETWEEN THE APOLOGY AND THE FORMULA

Luther indicated his approval of the AC and its *Apology*, and along with Melanchthon, increasingly emphasized the forensic nature of justification, distinguishing sanctification from it in order to make communication clearer in the wake of controversies and criticisms that arose after publication of these documents. Melanchthon also tried to precisely explain his view further in his *Romans Commentary* (1532) and his second edition of *Loci Communes* (1535).[11] In the *Romans Commentary* he says: "Paul develops his argument

---

8. Melanchthon, "Apology," 131.
9. Melanchthon, "Apology," 132.
10. Melanchthon, "Apology," 135.
11. Green, *How Melanchthon Helped Luther*, 235n46.

from the word 'imputing' and reasons clearly that our virtues are not worthy that God should approve them or pronounce them righteous, but that we are pronounced righteous through mercy, by divine imputation."[12] In his *Loci Communes* of 1535, he states: "The Hebrew word for justify is a forensic word . . . Abraham was pronounced righteous because he believed . . . not on account of his own worthiness [or the law], but on account of the mercy promised by God."[13]

In a letter replying to Johannes Brenz, Melanchthon urged a move away from an Augustinian view of justification, stating: "It is true that faith justifies, but not because it is the new work of the Holy Spirit within us [to fulfill the law] but because it grasps Christ." Luther added a postscript to this letter, writing: "try not to think of any quality in my heart such as faith or love, as it is called, but in their place I set Christ and say 'this is my righteousness.' Thus, he [Christ] says: 'I am the Way, the Truth, and the Life.' He does not say, 'I give you the way, the truth, and the life,' as if he were outside me and worked it within me. But these things should be, remain, and live not through me but in me."[14] This could be interpreted to both refer to imputation and to an indwelling Christ as one's righteousness—the whole Christ as a believer's possession.

ANDREAS OSIANDER THE ELDER: A DIFFERENT VIEW OF JUSTIFICATION

Osiander was a priest at the Augustinian monastery in Nuremberg and taught Hebrew there. He became a preacher at St. Lawrence Church where he introduced the Reformation, although independently and not as a pupil or follower of Luther. He had already come to his theological positions before meeting Luther in 1529. Then he became involved in controversy (with Melanchthon) over justification, after Luther's death. His Christology made a very sharp

---

12. Melanchthon, *CR*, 15:599 [Trans. Green, *How Melanchthon Helped Luther*, 226].

13. Melanchthon, *CR* 21:421 [Trans. Green, 227].

14. Luther, *CR* 2:503 [Trans. Green, 224].

distinction between the divine and human natures of Christ. According to Osiander it was the divine, not the human nature, that brought salvation. Unlike Luther and Melanchthon, he regarded atonement and justification as separate. Justification depended on the indwelling righteousness of Christ, made manifest by his Ascension, and it was thoroughly "analytic" in nature, being a divine verdict rendered on the inner transformation/sanctification of the believer. On October 24, 1550, Osiander published his *Disputation on Justification*. In it he attacked justification by imputation, and he was then accused of turning against Luther's teaching. He claimed to be faithful to Luther wherever scripture supported Luther. He was harsh in his condemnation of Melanchthon, whom he characterized as being like a "Judas of Iscariot." He rejected forensic justification. Melanchthon for his part acknowledged some of Osiander's points, especially pertaining to the indwelling of Christ. However, Melanchthon emphasized that it was the whole Christ that dwelled within, not only the divine nature, and that they couldn't be separated. Also, he reiterated that although Christ dwells within, "Nevertheless, much impurity, sinfulness, and lust remain in us all." In parallel fashion, the Atonement involved the dynamic (satisfaction) that existed between the human and divine natures, and therefore that Christ's work of atonement, which involved his human suffering, could not be separated from God's divine justification of sinners. Melanchthon related the indwelling, regeneration, and atonement in this way: "This is placed before us for our comfort, for also after our regeneration, again and again we must receive forgiveness of our sins and grace, for the sake of our mediator, Jesus Christ, through the merit of his obedience, by which he became the offering for us."[15] Osiander stimulated Melanchthon to explain Christ's role in redemption more clearly.

Instead of speaking only of God's imputation of righteousness for Christ's sake, after his conflict with Osiander, Melanchthon spoke of the imputation of Christ's own righteousness to the believer.[16] Specifically, it was Jesus Christ's obedience as a fully

---

15. Melanchthon, *CR* 7:895–896 [Trans. Green, 231].
16. Melanchthon, *CR* 15:1200 [Trans. Green, 230].

human being to God the Father that was imputed to the believer. This is what Osiander had vociferously denied.[17] Controversy over Osiander's teaching continued in very heated fashion, with sermons preached against him, and a chorale composed for congregations to sing that warned against "Osi's poison."[18] An amusing personal anecdote: I encountered a hymn based on this chorale in The *Lutheran Hymnal*[19] used in the Evangelical Lutheran Synodical Conference, and it was sung in a St. Paul, MN Missouri Synod congregation's worship service I attended in the early 1980s. It had the reference to Osi's poison in one verse, and I imagine the congregation sang it without having any idea what it was about.

The controversy was ultimately addressed in the FC as one of the theological disputes resolved to bring about confessional unity in the Lutheran churches after Luther (and later, Melanchthon) had passed from the scene.

THE *FORMULA OF CONCORD*

Theological disputes had arisen among the Wittenberg theologians in the form of six main controversies (Adiaphoristic, Majoristic, Osianderian, Synergistic, Eucharistic, and Original Sin). Under various stages of political pressure from the empire, they were motivated to try to reconcile and resolve their differences. They had generally coalesced into two opposing groups: the Philipists, who followed Melanchthon as their leading light; and the Gnesio-Lutherans, who claimed to strictly represent Luther's genuine original thought. The *Solid Declaration* of the *Formula of Concord* was the creation of a committee of post-Luther (and post-Melanchthon) theologians (Andrae, Chemnitz, Chrytraeus, and Seinecker) that worked on the resolution of controversies by addressing these issues in accord with (to be judged by) the Holy Scriptures, and as an adjunct to the (unaltered original) AC and

---

17. Chemnitz, "Judgment on Certain Controversies," 212.
18. Hirsch, *Theology of Andreas Osiander*.
19. *The Lutheran Hymnal*.

its *Apology*. They also pledged allegiance to both of Luther's catechisms. Each of the articles is presented in the form of a series of affirmative and negative theses, with the negative theses listing propositions condemned as false, contrary teaching to the preceding corresponding affirmative theses. Jakob Andrae shortened and summarized the content of the Solid Declaration for the territorial princes. This ended up as the *Epitome* section of the FC. The *Solid Declaration* was the full, expanded form produced by the committee. The final published version incorporated comments from feedback provided by theological correspondents that had been asked to review the text.

The discussion that follows here focuses on Article III *Concerning the Righteousness of Faith before God*. This article begins by dealing with the Osiandrian controversy, though Osiander is not explicitly named in the text of the article. It was the dispute that ultimately brought Philipists and Gnesio-Lutherans together in agreement (against him). It is also one that potentially has a bearing on the recent (twentieth century) Finnish school interpretation of Luther and on certain modern ecumenical discussions—for example, differing interpretations of the Council of Chalcedon and its Communicatio Idiomatum doctrine (communication of properties between the divine and human natures).

According to the *Epitome*, the chief question in this dispute is: "According to which nature is Christ our righteousness [divine or human]?" Affirmative thesis number one answers that it is both, i.e., the whole Christ, who rendered his obedience to the Father as both God and human being, earning forgiveness and eternal life for us. The article goes on to reiterate teachings about faith alone justifying, forgiveness of sin by sheer grace, reckoning the righteousness of Christ's obedience to the Christian believer, true trust in Christ (not mere knowledge), certainty of salvation, etc.[20] The *Solid Declaration* in this article said a little more about the disputing parties: "The one party argued that the righteousness of faith, which the apostle Paul calls the righteousness of God, is the

---

20. Kolb and Wengert, "Formula of Concord Epitome, Article III," in *The Book of Concord*, 494–97.

essential righteousness of God, that Christ himself (as the true, natural Son of God) is. He dwells in the elect through faith and impels them to do what is right . . . On the other hand, some have held and taught that Christ is our righteousness only according to his human nature." Osiander's idea reflected his neo-platonic training as a Hebraic humanist, while the human nature-only idea was constructed from formulations found in Peter Lombard's *Sentences*.[21] As mentioned before, both the Philipists and the Gnesio-Lutherans rejected these two formulations, although Jakob Andrae and Johannes Brenz tried to mediate the dispute by advocating some sympathy for Osiander's position. Ultimately it was decided that both natures in Christ constituted his righteousness for us.

The next chapter expresses some conclusions based on the analysis of previous chapters, after describing two important examples of contemporary, ecumenical issues in the theology of justification.

---

21. Kolb and Wengert, "Formula of Concord Epitome, Article III," in *The Book of Concord*, 562.

7

Ecumenical Considerations and Conclusions

THERE HAVE BEEN CERTAIN notable ecumenical re-appraisals of the classic Lutheran interpretation of justification. The following two subsections feature a discussion of two important examples, followed by another giving overall conclusions reached for this thesis.

THE NEW FINNISH LUTHER SCHOLARSHIP AND INTERPRETATION

What is called the Finnish school of Luther studies originated as an academic response on the Lutheran side to the Finnish Lutheran-Russian Orthodox theological dialog conducted beginning in the 1960s. Spearheading this effort was Tuomo Mannermma. Certain of his pupils at the University of Helsinki carried on the work and wrote extensively (after 1989), following his lead and advancing similar ideas. One of them produced a rigorous historical analysis of the doctrine of justification in Luther and the movement that followed in his wake up until 1580.[1]

---

1. Vainio, *Justification and Participation in Christ*.

Mannermaa says this: "According to Luther, justification is not merely a new ethical or juridical relation between God and a human being. When a human being believes in Christ, Christ is present, in the very fullness of his divine and human nature, in that faith itself."[2] This appears to be congruent with Luther's statements, and even with the writers of the FC who had disputed with Osiander by maintaining that both the divine and human natures indwelt the Christian believer, not only the divine (see my explanation in chapter 6). Mannermaa is critical of a "merely" forensic view, instead defending what has been called effective justification, which includes both God's favor and God's transformative gift to humans. The term captures the idea that God's Word, in this case the declaration of righteousness, is powerful to accomplish its intent, referring to the transformation. As such it is another way of incorporating sanctification into justification while seeming to give justification the theological priority in order. It also addresses the traditional Roman Catholic criticism that the Lutheran teaching on justification is weak and ineffective because it leaves people theoretically unchanged in their sinful state. Discussing Luther's larger *Galatians* commentary (1535), he goes on to say that justification and the real presence in faith are in danger of being separated by the dominance of the forensic interpretation, that both motifs (person and work) are united in Christ, and that this is identical with the righteousness of faith.

Mannermaa's participation in ecumenical dialogues, particularly with Russian Orthodox theologians, led to his accentuation of elements in Luther's writings that he found akin to the Orthodox doctrine of salvation through theosis (divinization). Kirsi Stjerna, former Professor of Church History at LTSG, and Manermaa's most prominent student living in the U.S., had this to say upon the occasion of his passing in 2015: "Professor Mannermaa in the 1980s introduced a hermeneutical paradigm shift in the reading of Luther's doctrine of justification by unfolding the centrality of the effective righteousness in Luther's theology of salvation . . . he discovered the under-appreciated dimension of Luther's central

---

2. Mannermaa, *Christ Present in Faith*, 87.

theology: the 'real-ontic' indwelling of Christ in faith, and the essential connection between love and faith. The ecumenical promise of the connections made between Luther's ideas of 'Christ present in faith' and the patristic notion of 'divinization' continues to generate new studies with different methodologies and premises." Robert Kolb was friendly with Mannermaa, strongly sharing the conviction with him that Luther's voice deserved to be heard across confessional boundaries. "Mannermaa's argument that the heart of the Wittenberg theology lay in Luther's adherence to theosis as an explanation of how God bestows righteousness upon sinners aroused discussion and returned researchers to the central question of the Reformation. The discussion has moved beyond his initial ideas, but the stimulus he has given has served the Church and scholarship in special ways. We thank the Lord for this friend." He was less sanguine about Mannermaa's actual views on justification: "Professor Mannermaa in fact was not advancing Osiander's ideas. But his interpretation of Luther's understanding of justification by faith came, in my opinion, perilously close by positing that the righteousness of the believer is a "real-ontic" righteousness infused by theosis, the "divinization" of the believer by the Holy Spirit through trust in Christ. Mannermaa had come to his conclusion on the basis of what I regarded as too few Luther texts as he was dialoging with theologians of the Russian Orthodox Church."[3]

"Divinization" is somewhat suspect and has been much debated, although there are precedents in theological history with church fathers, and even Luther's infrequent use of the term. The criticism is that it tends to confuse creator and creature. However, it refers specifically to becoming like God in terms of goodness rather than other, exclusively divine attributes. According to Mannermaa, Luther's references to ontological righteousness are theological rather than philosophical in nature, so that they don't lead

---

3. Kolb, et al., "Tuomo Mannermaa: Father of Finnish Interpretation of Luther Dies."

to a "theology of glory." They refer to union and "participation" with Christ.[4]

The Mannermaa school claims a continuity with ancient and medieval tradition, but in systematic terms, it is being tested in modern ecumenical relations. For example, beyond the Lutheran-Orthodox dialogs and rapprochement, effective and transformative ideas of justification and of union with Christ have reoriented Lutheran theology toward positions more acceptable and understandable for Catholic theologians as well. They were reportedly frequently discussed during the preparation and especially the revision of the JDDJ. Joseph Ratzinger (later, Pope Benedict) had an objection to the notion that one could be justified and a sinner at the same time, maintaining that if a person is not made righteous, they are not justified. The Annex to JDDJ says that the justified are "truly and inwardly renewed" and "do not remain sinners in this sense." However, they remain sinners in the sense that they have sinned. These different perspectives on justification have led to some criticism and backlash, naturally. Some have suspected that it is a revival of the Osiandrian view in somewhat different form. On the surface it looks like at least a partial lapse back into the Augustinian "inner renewal" motif for justification that Melanchthon battled and Luther moved away from in his mature phase. From the perspective of the *Lutheran Confessions*, it looks to me as though the distinction between justification and sanctification is being blurred again in the Finnish interpretation. But at the very least, there is a call to emphasize both aspects of God's action toward us more equally and together, which may not be a bad thing if kept in proper perspective, in a trinitarian framework.

Forensic justification has been dismissed by some as "legal fiction," and even "legalism." It has its defenders and partial defenders though (e.g., Gerhard O. Forde, Kurt E. Markquart, Robert Kolb, Mark Mattes, Lowell C. Green, Robert D. Brinsmead) and need not necessarily completely exclude real-ontological and effective dimensions. Luther himself was explicit about the nature of imputed righteousness. "Though sin remains, he considers us to

---

4. Saarinen, "Justification by Faith," 255.

be righteous and pure, and that a man is so absolved, as if he had no sin, for Christ's sake. We truly thank God, because his imputation is greater than our impurity."[5]

Some conservatives are concerned about a needless and deleterious departure from established and settled confessional doctrine. In the final paragraph of the FC, a commitment to the *Lutheran Confessions* was instituted that continued long afterward. "In it, we shall appear before the judgment throne of Jesus Christ, by God's grace, with fearless hearts and thus give an account of our faith, and we will neither secretly nor publicly speak or write anything contrary to it. Instead, on the strength of God's grace we intend to abide by this confession."[6] Echoes of this attitude could be seen well into the twentieth century, in the Confession of Faith articles in constitutions of Lutheran churches. In the American Lutheran Church (ALC), for example, there was a statement of unconditional subscription to the *Lutheran Confessions*: "The congregation accepts without reservation the symbolical books of the Evangelical Lutheran Church, not insofar as, but because they are the presentation and explanation of the pure doctrine of the Word of God and a summary of faith of the Evangelical Lutheran Church."[7] This sentence was dropped from the ALC's model constitution by 1984, and was not used in the ELCA (formed in 1987) constitution. Perhaps it is not wise to give a permanent unconditional allegiance to a written document, when theology changes and evolves through history. This puts the BC clearly and properly at a confessional level lower than the ancient ecumenical creeds and the scriptures.

Others have cited the advantages of the legal metaphor itself. Robert Brinsmead, a late Australian theologian, listed five logical negative consequences of neglecting the legal aspect of justification, as follows.[8]

5. LW 34:166.

6. Kolb and Wengert, "Formula of Concord Solid Declaration XII:40," in *The Book of Concord*, 656.

7. Constitution, Article II, 1.

8. Brinsmead, "Legal and Moral Aspects," 26–27.

Ecumenical Considerations and Conclusions

1. The crucifixion of Christ is emptied of real meaning if the sinner could be saved by moral renewal.
2. God's work in Christ is replaced by a work in man. Man, not God, becomes the center of religion.
3. The objective foundation for salvation is removed and replaced by subjectivism.
4. Sanctification is no longer based on justification, and therefore it is neither legal nor moral.
5. Such a repudiation of the legal aspects of redemption betrays the Protestant cause and loses the gifts of the Reformation.

One need not agree that all points in the above summary of the situation apply to the Finnish school completely. One doesn't need, either, to reject forensic justification as described in the FC. Those involved in its composition universally found it to be a great comfort to their consciences. It may very well be that the confessors neglected or chose not to highlight certain important aspects of Luther's views. If those are being rediscovered, established, and used to supplement confessional theology for the sake of enhancement and richness in understanding, that is beneficial. It is beyond the scope of this thesis to evaluate the Finnish school further, but in light of the way I have herein traced Luther's development and evolution regarding his thinking about justification, I would want to analyze which source texts were used by the Finns so as to determine whether their interpretations are more dependent on a particular phase of Luther's career. The Finnish school may have had some influence by advancing the idea that there can be new understandings and articulations of the doctrine of justification beyond historic confessional commitments, thereby opening more possibilities in ecumenical dialogs. Next, I discuss the historic agreement between the Lutheran World Federation (LWF) and the Roman Catholic Church as was achieved in the JDDJ. The Finnish school has had an influence on the LWF's work on it.

ONTOLOGICAL AND IMPUTED RIGHTEOUSNESS

THE *JOINT DECLARATION ON THE DOCTRINE OF JUSTIFICATION*

On October 31, 1999, representatives of the LWF and the Roman Catholic Church (the Pontifical Council for Promoting Christian Unity) signed a declaration of agreement on the understanding of salvation, which was the key conflict that had divided the churches during and since the Reformation. The JDDJ was the fruit and culmination of official ecumenical studies and dialog that has been taking place (since the Vatican II council came to a close in 1965) by theologians from both communions. An extensive series of topics were addressed in great detail by these studies, but the doctrine of justification was thought to be of greatest importance to resolve in an official declaration that summarized the dialog results on that subject. The specific studies on justification took place during phase III of the official dialogs, from 1983–1993. The conclusion emerged that the churches could go forward on common ground, overcoming and moving past their historic divisions. For Lutherans, this doctrine has been absolutely central—the most important of all—according to Luther, "the article on which the Church stands or falls." It was considered the "first and chief article"[9] of the Christian faith, the "ruler and judge over all other Christian doctrines."[10] It has not been as central to the Roman Catholic Church (the issue of ecclesiastical authority has generally been more central) but it has been recognized since the Council of Trent as the most neuralgic issue in the division from the Protestant point of view, and thus the most important to address and resolve for a move toward unity. Mutual condemnations were issued by both sides in the sixteenth century. With the signing of this document, those condemnations are stated not to apply to the partners when their teaching is in line with the current agreement. A convergence and basic consensus of shared understanding between them is thought to have been reached in the agreement as manifested in the JDDJ.[11]

---

9. Kolb and Wengert, "Smalcald Articles II:1," in *The Book of Concord*, 301.
10. *Luther's Works*, Weimar Edition (WA) 39–1:205 [trans. in the JDDJ, 7].
11. *JDDJ*, 11.

The JDDJ was able to assert that "By grace alone, in faith in Christ's saving work and not because of any merit on our part, we are accepted by God and receive the Holy Spirit, who renews our hearts while equipping and calling us to good works."

The document emphasizes both justifying and sanctifying grace, based on the saving work of Christ and the renewal (that activates love) wrought by the Holy Spirit. It acknowledges that justification has an essential and indispensable place in relation to all other Christian doctrines.[12] It also affirms that justification remains independent of that renewal or on human cooperation, though both aspects are joined in Christ, who is present in faith.[13] There remains a difference in perspective about sin remaining in the justified. The Catholic side still maintains that sin in the "proper sense" is completely taken away by baptism, and excludes concupiscence as actual sin. The common understanding between the two communions is that the Christian believer is no longer a slave to sin.[14]

Both Catholics and Lutherans say they can rely on the promises of God for salvation, in spite of human weakness. While from the Catholic side, a person should be concerned about his or her salvation, it is expressed as appropriate to trust that God intends salvation for them. Note that this has the same future hope orientation as was traditional in the medieval period, rather than the immediate, present assurance characteristic of Luther's reformational experience of salvation.[15] But it seems that there has been at least one remarkable result from this endeavor: historical misunderstandings of Luther's position as well as those of Johannes Eck and Thomas Aquinas have been cleared up, especially concerning the assurance of salvation. According to Sarah Hinlicky-Wilson, "Luther opposed Gabriel Biel's take as Pelagian, and due to his own limited knowledge extended this criticism to all other scholastic

---

12. *JDDJ*, 12.
13. *JDDJ*, 14–15.
14. *JDDJ*, 16.
15. *JDDJ*, 18.

theologians, including Thomas. But Thomas was as opposed to Biel's position as was Luther."[16]

In the JDDJ, we find this: "With the Second Vatican Council, Catholics state: to have faith is to entrust oneself totally to God, who liberates us from the darkness of sin and death and awakens us to eternal life."[17] This is no longer mere intellectual assent to facts about salvation or to the authority of official Catholic teaching. The debt to Luther is obvious. "The outcome, then, of many decades of Lutheran-Catholic dialogue was not only to remove one of the misunderstandings that had dogged their relations for nearly five centuries. It was to discover the great extent to which Catholics could willingly share Lutheran concerns and convictions, even to the point of revising their own past formulations, such as the definition of faith, in line with Lutheran teaching."[18] Forensic justification was not mentioned directly in the main text, but was mentioned as follows in a footnote that referenced a source document used in the composition of section 3, titled *The Common Understanding of Justification*: "A faith-centered and forensically conceived picture of justification is of major importance for Paul and, in a sense, for the Bible as a whole, although it is by no means the only biblical or Pauline way of representing God's saving work."[19]

At the conclusion of the JDDJ, and in the *Official Common Statement*, it is made clear that the mutual condemnations of the sixteenth century don't apply to the teaching about justification as understood in the framework of the agreement made in the JDDJ. The historical Lutheran confessional documents and the decrees of the Council of Trent are not abrogated (they still remain valid as warnings of theological boundaries), but are effectively put to the side in the interest of proceeding together on common ground rather than re-litigating controversies of the past. The current teachings on justification represented by the JDDJ are not

16. Wilson, "Six Ways Ecumenical Progress Is Possible," 314.
17. *JDDJ*, 18.
18. Wilson, "Six Ways Ecumenical Progress Is Possible," 314.
19. *JDDJ*, 21.

considered church-dividing, but are deemed acceptable to both sides.

It is unclear overall what Church reception ultimately will be. It seems like the spirit of ecumenism had waned in the Roman Catholic Church during the conservative papacies of John Paul II and Benedict XVI. Professional ecumenists including Susan K. Wood and associates within the American Catholic Church complained of their frustration to me privately when they visited United Lutheran Seminary (ULS) for a conference. They expressed the hope that Pope Francis would live long enough to revive ecumenism in the Catholic Church. At my seminary (LTSG, now ULS) the JDDJ was addressed as part of the *Lutheran Confessions* course. It seems to be treated as a quasi-confessional document that supplements or supersedes parts of the BC in ways. At the very least, it is an extra-confessional document that is treated with respect and serious consideration in the ELCA and in various national church bodies of the LWF. But like so many things, time will tell. Openness to any continuing future genuine dialog can only be good. Other worldwide communions of Christian denominations have since signed on to the JDDJ, including Anglican, Reformed, and Methodist, so it's quite a broad representation of churches.

An important issue raised by the JDDJ is whether the price of such an agreement impacts confessional integrity and compromises theological identity. I attended the public session at Notre Dame University in March 2019, following a consultation of all five communions that had signed as parties to the JDDJ. During the Q&A following the presentation by the representatives for the consultation, I raised this very question about implications for confessional identity. The first response to my question came from Rev. Dr. Martin Junge, at that time serving as General Secretary of the LWF. He said that the purpose of ecumenical theological dialog was not to blur or sideline confessional identity or a legitimate measure of commitment to our history. Rather, it was to facilitate better understanding and find common ground in good faith and goodwill, where there may have been unwarranted hostility, misunderstanding, and condemnations in the past. According to

Junge, we should aim to bring our full identities to the table, so to speak, in the interest of finding what unity may be achieved. The importance of rescinding the historic mutual condemnations and anathemas is that the different Christian communions can be freed from always maintaining a defensive posture, Junge said. Instead, they can be open to the contributions and insights that each is able to offer. The second response came from Rev. Dr. Chris Ferguson, General Secretary of the World Communion of Reformed Churches. He pointed out that the Lutheran churches effectively have a single confession of faith, or rather an established set of official documents (closely related to the original AC) that have been used unchanged since 1580. The Reformed churches have taken a different approach by producing a great number of confessions of faith at different times and places, each being more particular to a specific situation. One of these adopted is the *Barmen Declaration*, which was written as recently as 1934, in the midst of the rise of Nazism in Germany. He recommended this approach to doing theology, perhaps implying that the JDDJ could be considered an official new confession of faith to be adopted by contemporary churches—at least by the five signatories—for the communions represented at the consultation.

CONCLUSIONS

There is not necessarily a disparity between being pronounced righteous (imputation) and in actually being righteous (ontological) if justification is equated with the forgiveness of sin. The forgiven sinner is no longer guilty; he or she is just and righteous. In this view, although the believer is still a sinner by nature in himself or herself, that person is simultaneously a saint, i.e., righteous in God's sight, based on the righteousness of Christ as the mediator, substitute, and representative.

In this thesis, I have attempted to trace the beginning, turning point, development, and final confessional expression of the Lutheran reformational doctrine of justification. Historically, the posting of the *Ninety-Five Theses* in October 1517 is considered the beginning of the Reformation. However, the content of the theses could be considered theologically orthodox and conventional even from the medieval Roman Catholic point of view. The evangelical reformers questioned the penitential system and the legitimacy of indulgences as practiced rather than in theory. It was abuses Luther first objected to, as well as then-current assumptions about extent of the Pope's authority over the afterlife (purgatory) and by extension, the Church's jurisdiction of same. Questioning the spiritual authority of the Roman Catholic Church is what got him into trouble and drew him further into conflict. Luther remained confident that the Pope would support him if only he became aware of the extent of abuses. This proved to be spectacularly wrong. As Luther engaged in conflict and polemics with church authorities, he also began questioning the theology he had inherited from his teachers. This was aided and abetted by humanists such as Erasmus, who spearheaded a movement of "back to the sources," including examining the biblical texts in the original languages. These intellectual forces and Luther's curiosity combined with an intense psychological and emotional crisis he manifested—what was called anfechtung. He was worried about his salvation and how he might be accepted and loved by God, to achieve a right standing (justification) in the here and now. He experienced himself deeply as a sinner, and his conscience was not quieted and comforted by the medieval church's prescriptions. He was on a quest for a gracious God, and eventually found what he was looking for in the scriptures (especially in Paul's epistles and in the *Psalms*) as he studied and taught courses as a professor at Wittenberg University.

Recent attempts (twentieth century) have been made to analyze, date, and identify the critical theological turning point for the Reformation in Luther's lectures, sermons, and writings. Some scholars have emphasized a turning point or "eureka" moment in Luther's theology along with claims to have dated it more or less precisely by looking at the documentary evidence for a historical change in Luther's use of language to explain theological concepts. This has been problematic, especially since the renaissance in

Luther studies in the 1950s, 1960s, and beyond. To cite one example: the popular but erroneous attempt to date the evangelical discovery before 1517, under the assumption that the *Ninety-Five Theses* were the result rather than the cause of Luther's reformational change in thinking. His earlier writings were analyzed for clues concentrating on works such as his commentaries on *Romans* and the *Psalms*, either without a clear understanding or a fair (objective) treatment of his most important later insights and the Reformation's fundamental meaning with regard to the doctrine of justification. That situation has been remedied in recent decades (post-1970) as many scholars have turned to give more attention to Luther's later writings and more credence to his own recollections. Since then, some who have argued for a later dating (mid-1518 to 1519) include: Uuras Saarnivaara, Oswald Bayer, Kurt Aland, Martin Brecht, and Carter Lindberg. Many others could be named.

Analysis of historiographical data (by Oswald Bayer and others) suggests that the change was initiated by the realization of immediate salvation to anyone who believes and embraces God's promise of forgiveness to the sinner for Christ's sake—in other words that it is faith, defined as trust, that justifies. This appears in Luther's writing consistently from late 1518 onwards, and represents the first documented reformational idea—the first definitive departure from established Catholic doctrine on the subject of justification. That isn't the end of the story, though. It took several years for the consequences of that discovery to work itself out in a coherent set of teachings that mark a fully reformational theology. Scholars such as Berndt Hamm and Bernhard Lohse focused their attention not on a single turning point, but on a succession of stages of development. These stages unfolded as Luther and his close colleague Philip Melanchthon defended their ideas during conflict and controversy, and as they gradually extricated themselves mentally from the medieval scholastic milieu from which they had emerged.

These two characterizations of Luther's process of discovery are not contradictory or exclusive. The two turning points, described later in life by Luther himself, are instructive. His recollection of the tower experience in 1545 reads like an emotional or psychological turning point. His breakthrough in this way consisted in a new understanding of Paul's usage of the term "righteousness of God" as gift of grace given to the believer rather than what he had previously understood to be a reference to divine judgment. This was what relieved him of his experience of anfechtung. As evidence for this, in his recounting he says "Here I felt that I was altogether born again and had entered paradise itself through open gates."[20] In another recollection, he cited his realization of the distinction between law and gospel as his great theological turning point: "But when I discovered the proper distinction—namely, that the law is one thing and the gospel is another—I made myself free."[21] I interpret this to be his intellectual turning point for biblical studies, greater understanding, and more effective theological explanations. This is where both his turning point and his step-by-step development in stages make sense taken together as a whole trajectory. One thing motivated and initiated the other, as Luther attempted to translate his experience and discoveries into effective teaching and reform of the Church.

The shape and response of justification through faith alone, by grace alone, for the sake of Christ alone was conditioned by Luther's experience of the penitential system and its built-in uncertainty, which made salvation a fearful hope for future divine acceptance rather than a present comforting assurance. Once Luther (with Melanchthon's assistance) had worked out a purely passive, objective, extrinsic righteousness, he no longer felt the anxiety of wondering whether the inner transformation wrought by the Holy Spirit was thorough and complete enough to warrant God's positive verdict for him at judgment. Faith was then understood to be perfect and sufficient to render persons righteous in God's eyes, while the inner transformation to holiness, and the fruit of good works that necessarily followed from being justified, were real and good, yet still imperfect in this mortal life. Luther came to maintain that believers both remained sinners and were at the same

---

20. LW 34:337.
21. LW 54:443.

time justified simply because God declared it and made it so out of pure love and mercy.

After the first stage of understanding God's work of imparting righteousness, Luther went on to realize (with Melanchthon's help) in a subsequent stage that the traditional (and Augustinian) view was that although it was God's grace that justified, it happened through a process of inner renewal, healing, transformation, and cooperation on the part of the human person. It was something that needed to be perfected with more grace in synergistic fashion, until final realization of the hope of salvation at the end of life. The next stage for Luther was to understand that faith itself was righteousness, rather than spiritual performance, active cooperation, or works. Finally, with Melanchthon, he came to the understanding that it was Christ's own righteousness of perfect obedience to the Father that was imputed to the Christian believer through faith. Luther cited this realization in the concluding sentence of his recollection of the tower experience. "Later I read Augustine's *On the Spirit and the Letter*, where . . . I found that he, too, interpreted God's righteousness in a similar way . . . Although this was heretofore said imperfectly and he did not explain all things concerning imputation clearly."[22]

God's righteousness was identified with forgiveness of sin and Christ's atoning work. He had essentially arrived at what is known as a forensic understanding of justification—the declaration of acquittal as in the courtroom metaphor used by Paul. This was eventually enshrined, after resolution of certain controversies (as with Osiander), in the *Lutheran Confessions*, as the standard Lutheran view of justification. It should be kept in mind, however, that this is a metaphor and one interpretation of the doctrine, though it may be the dominant one for Protestants historically. Luther felt free at times to use other metaphors, depending on the situation, if he thought they better communicated the gospel in context. What was most important to him was the actual lived experience of forgiveness and reconciliation with God, more than the explanation of how it happens.

22. LW 34:337.

There have been challenges to a purely forensic understanding, but Luther makes this important point in his 1531–35 *Lectures on Galatians*: "These two things perfect Christian righteousness. One is heartfelt faith (trust) that is a divinely given gift and formally believes in Christ . . . Faith is indeed a formal righteousness, but it is not enough because even after faith remnants of sin still cling to the flesh . . . The second part of righteousness is . . . the divine imputation . . . God's reckoning this imperfect faith as perfect righteousness for the sake of Christ . . . who has suffered for the sins of the world."[23]

---

23. LW 26:229, 231.

Bibliography

Anderson, Jeffrey K. *Justification as Speech of the Spirit: A Pneumatological and Trinitarian Approach to Forensic Justification.* Eugene, OR: Wipf & Stock, 2021.
Arand, Charles P., James A. Nestingen, and Robert Kolb. *The Lutheran Confessions: History and Theology of The Book of Concord.* Minneapolis: Fortress, 2012.
Augustine, *On the Spirit and the Letter.* Translated by W. J. Sparrow Simpson. New York: Macmillan, 1925.
Aulén, Gustav. *Christus Victor: An Historical Study of the Three Main Types of the Idea of Atonement* (1931). Translated by A.G. Herbert. Reprint, Eugene, OR: Wipf and Stock, 2003.
———. *The Faith of the Christian Church.* 2nd English ed. Translated by Eric H. Wahlstrom. Philadelphia: Fortress, 1960.
Bainton, Roland. *Here I Stand: A Life of Martin Luther.* New York: Abingdon-Cokesbury, 1950.
Bayer, Oswald. *Living by Faith: Justification and Sanctification.* 2nd ed. 1990. Translated by Geoffrey W. Bromily. 2002. Lutheran Quarterly Books Reprint, Minneapolis: Fortress, 2017.
———. *Martin Luther's Theology: A Contemporary Interpretation.* 3rd ed. Translated by Thomas H. Trapp. Grand Rapids, MI: Eerdmans, 2008.
Brinsmead, Robert D. "The Legal and Moral Aspects of Salvation Part 2." *Present Truth* 5.5 (1976) 20–30
Cary, Phillip. *The Meaning of Protestant Theology: Luther, Augustine, and the Gospel That Gives Us Christ.* Grand Rapids, MI: Baker Academic, 2019.
Catechism of the Catholic Church. 2nd ed. (with modifications from the editio typica). Translated by the United States Catholic Conference–Libreria Editrice Vaticana. New York: Doubleday, 1997.
Chemnitz, Martin. "Judgement on Certain Controversies Concerning Certain Articles of the Augsburg Confession Which Have Recently Arisen and Caused Controversy." In *Sources and Contexts of the Book of Concord*, edited by Robert Kolb and James A. Nestigen, 197–219. Minneapolis: Fortress, 2001.

BIBLIOGRAPHY

Chung, Yong-Seok. "Martin Luther and the Scholastics on Justification." *Korea Journal of Christian Studies* 48 (2013). https://koreanchristianity.cdh.ucla.edu/.

Constitution for Faith Lutheran Church of Castro Valley, CA, Article II (1960).

Crump, Eric. Review of "Defending Faith: Lutheran Responses to Andreas Osiander's Doctrine of Justification 1551–9" by Timothy Wengert. *Seminary Ridge Review* 15.2 (Spring 2013) 94–100.

Dictionary of Luther and the Lutheran Traditions. Edited by Timothy J. Wengert et al. Grand Rapids: Baker Academic, 2017.

Dingle, Irene. "The Debate Over Justification in Ecumenical Dialog." *Lutheran Quarterly* 15.3 (Autumn 2001) 293–316.

Dragseth, Jennifer Hockenbery. *The Devil's Whore: Reason and Philosophy in the Lutheran Tradition.* Minneapolis: Fortress, 2011.

———. "Spirit and Letter, Gospel and Law: Augustine and Luther in Conversation." *Seminary Ridge Review* 18.2 (Spring 2016) 16–34.

Elert, Werner. "Humanitat und kirche. Zum 450. Geburtstag Melanchthon." *Zwischen gnade und ungnade: Abwandlungen des themas gesetz und evangelium.* Munich: Evangelischer Presserverbund fur Bayern, 1948.

Erasmus, Desiderius. *On Copia of Words and Ideas.* Edited and translated by Donald B. King and H. David Ricks. Milwaukee: Marquette University Press, 1963.

Evangelical Lutheran Worship. Minneapolis: Augsburg Fortress, 2007.

Forde, Gerhard O. *The Essential Forde: Distinguishing Law and Gospel.* Edited by Mark C. Mattes and Steven D. Paulson. Lutheran Quarterly Books. Minneapolis: Fortress, 2019.

———. *Justification by Faith—A Matter of Death and Life.* Philadelphia: Fortress, 1982.

———. *The Law-Gospel Debate: An Interpretation of its Historical Development.* Minneapolis: Augsburg, 1969.

———. *A More Radical Gospel: Essays on Eschatology, Authority, Atonement, and Ecumenism.* Edited by Mark C. Mattes and Steven D. Paulson. Lutheran Quarterly Books Reprint, Minneapolis: Fortress, 2017.

From Conflict to Communion: Lutheran-Catholic Common Commemoration of the Reformation in 2017. Report of the Lutheran-Roman Catholic Commission on Unity. Leipzig: Evangelische Verlagsanstalt and Bonifatius, 2013.

Gassmann, Gunther, and Scott Hendrix. *Fortress Introduction to the Lutheran Confessions.* Minneapolis: Fortress, 1999.

Gerrish, Brian A. *The Old Protestantism and the New: Essays on the Reformation Heritage.* Reprint, London: T&T Clark International, 2004.

Graybill, Gregory B. *The Honeycomb Scroll: Phillipp Melanchthon at the Dawn of the Reformation.* Minneapolis, Fortress, 2015.

Green, Lowell C. *How Melanchthon Helped Luther Discover the Gospel: The Doctrine of Justification in the Reformation.* Fallbrook, CA: Verdict, 1980.

———. "The Influence of Erasmus upon Melanchthon, Luther, and the Formula of Concord." *Church History* 43 (June 1974) 183–200.

Bibliography

Gritsch, Eric W. *A History of Lutheranism*. Minneapolis: Fortress, 2002.

Hamm, Berndt. *The Early Luther: Stages in a Reformation Reorientation*. Translated by Martin J. Lormann. Lutheran Quarterly Books Reprint, Minneapolis: Fortress, 2017.

Hillerbrand, Hans J., et al., eds. *The Annotated Luther*. Vols. 1–6. Minneapolis: Fortress, 2015–17.

Hirsch, Emmanuel. *The Theology of Andreas Osiander and Its Historical Prerequisites*. 1919. https://www.deutsche-digitale-bibliothek.de.

Iwand, Hans J. *The Righteousness of Faith According to Luther*. Edited by Virgil F. Thompson. Translated by Randi H. Lundell. Eugene, OR: Wipf & Stock, 2008.

Joint Declaration on the Doctrine of Justification, 20th Anniversary Edition, by the Lutheran World Federation and the Roman Catholic Church, (including statements from the World Methodist Council, the Anglican Consultative Council, and the World Communion of Reformed Churches). Geneva: The Lutheran World Federation, 2019.

Keith, Scott L. Preface to *How Melanchthon Helped Luther Discover the Gospel* by Lowell C. Green. Reprint, Irvine, CA: 1517, 2021.

Kolb, Robert. *Andreae and the Formula of Concord: Six Sermons on the Way to Lutheran Unity*. St. Louis: Concordia, 1977.

———. "Contemporary Lutheran Understandings of the Doctrine of Justification: A Selective Glimpse." In *Justification: What's at Stake in the Current Debates?*, edited by Mark Husbands and Daniel Trier, 153–76. Downers Grove, IL: Intervarsity, 2004.

Kolb, Robert, et al., eds. *The Oxford Handbook of Martin Luther's Theology*. Oxford: Oxford University Press, 2014.

Kolb, Robert, and James A. Nestingen, eds. *Sources and Contexts of the Book of Concord*. Minneapolis: Fortress, 2001.

Kolb, Robert, and Timothy J. Wengert, eds. *The Book of Concord: The Confessions of the Evangelical Lutheran Church*. Translated by Charles Arand et al. Minneapolis: Fortress, 2000.

Leppin, Volker. "Introduction to the Bondage of the Will." In *The Annotated Luther, Vol. 2: Word and Faith*, 153–57. Minneapolis: Fortress, 2015.

Lohse, Bernhard. *Martin Luther's Theology: Its Historical and Systematic Development*. Edited and translated by Roy A. Harrisville. Minneapolis: Fortress, 1999.

Lull, Timothy F., and William R. Russell, eds. *Martin Luther's Basic Theological Writings*. 3rd ed. Minneapolis: Fortress, 2012.

Luther, Martin. (various articles), in *Corpus Reformatorum Vol. 2*.

———. "Lectures on Romans 3:20–27." In *The Annotated Luther, Vol. 6: The Interpretation of Scripture*, translated by Piotr J. Malysz, 485–500. Minneapolis: Fortress, 2017.

MacCulloch, Diarmaid. *Christianity: The First 3000 Years*. New York: Viking Penguin, 2010.

BIBLIOGRAPHY

Mannermaa, Tuomo. *Christ Present in Faith*. Translated and Edited by Kirsi Stjerna. Minneapolis: Fortress, 2005.

Marty, Myron A. *Lutherans and Roman Catholicism: The Changing Conflict 1917-63*. Notre Dame, IN: University of Notre Dame Press, 1968.

McGonigle, Herbert. "Augustine v Pelagius on Original Sin." *European Explorations in Christian Holiness* 2 (Summer 2001) 43–54.

Melanchthon, Philip. (various articles), in *Corpus Reformatorum 1834*. Vols. 7, 15, 21.

Melanchthon, Philip. *Loci Communes Theologici*. Translated by Lowell J. Satre with revisions by Wilhelm Pauck. *Library of Christian Classics, Vol. 19: Melanchthon and Bucer*. Philadelphia: Westminster Press, 1969.

Murphy, Lawrence F. "Martin Luther and Gabriel Biel: A Disagreement about Original Sin." *Science et espirit* 32.1 (1980) 52–72.

Oberman, Heiko. *The Harvest of Medieval Theology: Gabriel Biel and Late Medieval Nominalism*. Cambridge, MA: Harvard University Press, 1963.

Pelikan, Jaroslav, and Helmut Lehmann, eds. *Luther's Works*, American Edition, Vols. 1–55. St. Louis: Concordia and Minneapolis: Fortress, 1955–86.

Rex, Richard. *The Making of Martin Luther*. Princeton, NJ: Princeton University Press, 2017.

Saarinen, Risto. "Justification by Faith: The View of the Mannermaa School." In *The Oxford Handbook of Luther's Theology*, 254–63. Oxford: Oxford University Press, 2014.

Saarnivaara, Uuras. *Luther Discovers the Gospel: New Light upon Luther's Way from Medieval Catholicism to Evangelical Faith*. English ed. St. Louis: Concordia, 2005.

Stendahl, Krister. "The Apostle Paul and the Introspective Conscience of the West." *Harvard Theological Review* 56. Cambridge, MA: Cambridge University Press, 1963.

Stjerna, Kirsi I. *Lutheran Theology: A Grammar of Faith*. London: T&T Clark, 2021.

The Lutheran Hymnal. St. Louis: Concordia, 1941.

Tornau, Christian. "Augustine of Hippo." In *The Stanford Encyclopedia of Philosophy*, edited by Edward N. Zalta and Uri Nodelman. Accessed April 26, 2024. https://plato.stanford.edu/entries/augustine/.

"Tuomo Mannermaa: Father of Finnish Interpretation of Luther Dies." Concordia Theology, Jan. 21, 2015. https://concordiatheology.org/2015/01/tuomo-mannermaa-father-of-finnish-interpretation-of-luther-dies/.

Vainio, Olli-Pekka. *Justification and Participation in Christ: The Development of the Lutheran Doctrine of Justification from Luther to the Formula of Concord (1580)*. Leiden, Netherlands: Brill, 2008.

Wengert, Timothy J. *Defending Faith: Lutheran Responses to Andreas Osiander's Doctrine of Justification, 1551–9*. Studies in the Late Middle Ages, Humanism, and the Reformation 65. Tübingen: Mohr Siebeck, 2012.

BIBLIOGRAPHY

Whalen, William J. *Separated Brethren: A Survey of Protestant, Anglican, Eastern Orthodox and Other Denominations in the United States.* 3rd ed. Huntington, IN: Our Sunday Visitor, Inc., Bruce, 1979.

What Luther Says: A Practical In-Home Anthology for the Active Christian. Compiled by Ewald M. Plass. St. Louis: Concordia, 1959.

Wilson, Sarah Hinlicky. "Six Ways Ecumenical Progress Is Possible." *Concordia Journal,* Fall 2013.

Wood, Susan K., and Timothy J. Wengert. *A Shared Spiritual Journey: Lutherans and Catholics Traveling Toward Unity.* New York: Paulist, 2016.

Yule, George, ed. *Luther: Theologian for Catholics and Protestants.* Edinburgh: T&T Clark, 1985.

www.ingramcontent.com/pod-product-compliance
Lightning Source LLC
Chambersburg PA
CBHW072010090426
42734CB00033B/2379